CRIMSON & GOLD:
THE DENVER PIONEERS'
MAGICAL RUN TO THE
2004 NATIONAL CHAMPIONSHIP

Pat Rooney

KCI SPORTS VENTURES

SAVOY, IL

ISBN: 0-9758769-0-2
Library of Congress Number: Applied for

KCI Sports Ventures, LLC
1402 Quail Run Drive
Savoy, IL 61874

Editor: Peter J. Clark
Coordinating Editor: Molly C. Voorheis
Dustjacket Design: Terry Neutz-Hayden
Book Layout and Design: Erich J. Bacher

Photos Courtesy of William R. Sallaz (www.ActionPic9.com), Monty Rand Photography, Kevin Ferguson, Charlie Lengal III, Tom Kimmell, De Frisco Photography, Sandy Hubbard, Scott O'Neil, *Rocky Mountain News,* University of North Dakota Athletics, University of Miami (Ohio) Media Relations, University of Minnesota-Duluth Media Relations, University of Denver Office of Communications and Marketing, University of Denver Media Relations and The White House Office of Media and Public Affairs.

Articles reprinted with permission of *Rocky Mountain News.*

Printing and binding done by Worzalla Publishing, Stevens Point, WI.

The publisher would like to offer a special thanks to the following for their continued support of University of Denver Athletics. Without them this book would not be possible.

The Burnsley Hotel
CIBER
Comcast
The Pepsi Bottling Group
Fox Sports Net Rocky Mountain
KKFN 950 "The Fan"
Players Bench
Channel 9 KUSA
University of Denver Alumni Association
Great Northern Tavern
Marriott
Moray and Pamela Keith
University of Denver Bookstore
University of Denver
Division of Athletics and Recreation
Wells Fargo Private Client Services

Table of Contents

Acknowledgements

My gratitude goes out to head coach George Gwozdecky, Erich Bacher, and the University of Denver athletic administration and student-athletes for their cooperation with this project. Thanks to Peter Clark for making it happen and to Molly for always being there when I need to vent and when I need to laugh.

-- P.R.

The publisher would like to recognize and offer a "very special thank you" to the following for their efforts in making this book a reality:

Head Coach George Gwozdecky, his staff and the Pioneer players - without your outstanding efforts there wouldn't be a book.

Dr. M. Dianne Murphy and the entire University of Denver athletic administration for their assistance and support of this book.

Jon Boos and Rob Revitte for their suggestions and guidance.

Erich Bacher and Terry Neutz-Hayden for their friendship, long hours of work and talented layout and design abilities - great job and thank you guys.

Pat Rooney for recapturing the excitement of a magical season.

The many skilled photographers who contributed photos to this project.

Bret Kroencke for helping steer the ship in the right direction.

Kim Deuel and the neighborhood crew at Worzalla Publishing for all of their hard work in getting the book out on time.

-- Peter Clark
Publisher

Foreword

I stood in the same spot in the reserved suite at the FleetCenter as the other NCAA committee members, trying to be impartial, but as the chair of the committee, it wasn't easy. My emotions were inescapable. Being an old goalie, I had moved to the sanctum of this prime real estate from the time we were down 3-1 in the semifinals. I had experienced these circumstances as a player in 1973 when we lost in the finals in the exact same city, Boston, and as an assistant coach in 1986 when we lost both games in the Final Four just down the interstate in Providence. And now, as an administrator in the Athletic Department, I had watched this hockey team compete all year. They had mourned the loss of former players and felt the ambivalence of a losing streak in the new year. Making the playoffs was always the goal, but winning two consecutive games was more immediate. Their character never wavered, and they battled together with one common emotion…pride.

In the stands, alumni and supporters comprised just a fraction of the crowd, but their enthusiasm was apparent. From the suite, I could see two guys dressed in togas leading the cheers as they had in the "old barn." I was just waiting to see the chickens come over the glass. I saw former players, some who had "unfinished business," and others whose gray hair resembled mine. There were administrators whose visions for the future stood as tall as the new landscape at DU, and those who reminisced about the good old days. There were parents nervously pacing behind the seats, and there were friends and families, shaking their pom poms. The scoreboard read 1-0. As the clock slowly ticked down, the collective tension mounted. Maine fans screamed for a tie; DU fans cheered for a victory. And then we all heard the ref's whistle blow. The infraction called against DU…not once, but twice. It couldn't be.

I've always said it is easier to play than watch. And that's just what the players did. They played the rest of the game as if refusing to lose…even 6-on-3 (or four, don't forget the goalie). As those last seconds ticked off the clock, I was behind the benches waiting to present the trophy to the winner. And there was only one team I wanted to present it to…my alma mater. When the scoreboard clock finally showed 0:00, the feeling was almost surreal. I've been described as a pretty quiet man, but at that moment I jumped and hugged the first person I saw. The players were jubilant. The fans were exultant. That's what winning should feel like.

Nowadays, TV dictates the timing of many major sporting events, so everyone hustled to get a few pictures for the highlight reels. But as soon as that was over, I moved quickly to congratulate the boys. One by one they came forward, and I presented them their watches. Their smiles were reflected in my face, and their excitement and pride was cheered from our section of screaming fans.

A few weeks have gone by, and I've tried to put into perspective what this championship has meant. The team has been honored by many, including Governor Bill Owens, President George W. Bush and Denver's professional sports teams. Congratulations have come in the form of handshakes, phone calls and e-mails. But the impact of this championship is far greater than this moment, spanning the course of the last 35 years.

This championship connects DUs last championship in 1969 to the current program and truly validates the tradition of DU hockey. It unites everyone who has ever been a part of DU hockey, including those who won, those who lost, those who donned the crimson and gold for one minute or for a full game. It recognizes the trainers who logged a thousand hours and the fans who called DU their team. It honors those voices who described the action each and every game and those who we pay tribute to with awards in their names. It memorializes legendary coaches and legendary stories about the 9th Hole and the Border. This championship captures the spirit of this program…DU pride.

Ron Grahame

Ron Grahame
University of Denver Associate Athletics Director
Pioneer Hockey Letterwinner 1970-73

Prologue

For the Team...
For the Journey...
For the Event...

It was 3 a.m. in the heart of the holiday season, and the only thing stirring in the house shared by five University of Denver hockey players was the surreal digital glow created by video games and a computer screen.

Ryan Caldwell and fellow senior Scott McConnell were playing an early-morning game in a ritual that has become a form of meditation to the modern college student. The two Pioneer players were venting some of their competitive fire while also relaxing following the grind of classes, now on hiatus for the holidays.

Caldwell, the team captain, owed much of his insomnia to the issues surrounding his team. They were vexing, this group of Pioneers. They could go on the road and dominate some of the best teams in the country. Yet on their home ice they often skated like high school kids. The conundrum was driving Caldwell mad. Until they figured it out, the team ultimately would waste its talent.

A few days earlier the Pioneers completed an impressive sweep at St. Cloud State, leaving the team in fifth place in the rugged Western Collegiate Hockey Association (WCHA). Only their perplexing inconsistency was keeping the Pioneers from charging to the top of the standings. The Pioneers had yet to record a WCHA win at home, tarnishing some of the luster of the impressive wins they had collected on the road.

Caldwell was sharp enough to recognize that his teammates were still trying to discover the style of play that would suit them best. The team was blessed with line after line of offensive talent, yet their most impressive wins to that point occurred when the Pioneers shut the door defensively.

Caldwell noodled with the controls of the video game. The mantra of the team, a mission statement accidentally bestowed upon the Pioneers by one of the program's biggest heroes, Keith Magnuson, rattled through his head.

For the Team...
For the Journey...
For the Event...

Caldwell was giving his all for a team that had only just begun what would become an inexplicable journey. During a visit with the team two months earlier, Magnuson told his beloved Pioneers to steel themselves for The Event, a mysterious crossroads they would recognize once the journey carried them there. They would know they were in The Event when it happened. Caldwell may have wondered exactly what sort of dramatic moment was awaiting the Pioneers when a blank-faced McConnell suddenly beckoned his roommate to the computer screen.

"I said, 'Hey dude, you gotta see this,'" recalls McConnell. "I looked at the news and it was denial right away."

What McConnell saw was the first news reports of a car accident outside Toronto earlier that day that had claimed Magnuson's life.

Senior Scott McConnell was one of the first Pioneers to hear about the tragic death of former Denver great Keith Magnuson.

William R. Sallaz

Before embarking on a 12-year career with the Chicago Blackhawks, Magnuson had been a standout defenseman for the University of Denver, leading the storied Pioneers program to back-to-back national championships in 1968 and 1969. So significant was his impact on the college game that Magnuson, one of DU's captains in 1969, was named to the NCAA's 50th anniversary team in 1997.

Magnuson prospered in the NHL, spending a season and a half as Chicago's head coach once his playing days were over, yet Denver's program never left Magnuson's heart. He was a fixture at Denver alumni games, and he tried to visit the Pioneers' locker room a few times every season. Magnuson never failed to make a lasting impression, as he did when he led the victory party following Denver's championship in the 2002 WCHA Final Five.

"When we won the WCHA Final Five he came down and was just revved up," senior Connor James said. "He wasn't just high-fiving everyone. He was hugging everyone. He came down and met everyone earlier in the year. Even with the freshmen, when he gave you a handshake he looked in your eyes and he knew who you were. He followed Pioneer hockey compulsively. For someone that well-respected not only in college hockey, but in the NHL, that's special. When he passed away it was a huge blow to a lot of guys."

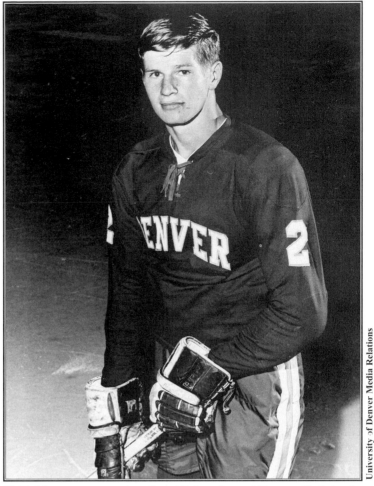

Keith Magnuson was a two-time All-American at Denver. He helped the Pioneers to back-to-back NCAA championships in 1968 and 1969. Magnuson played 12 seasons with the NHL's Chicago Blackhawks.

University of Denver Media Relations

Magnuson's untimely death would send shockwaves through the hockey world. Yet the tremors seemed rooted at the base of the Rocky Mountains, where the Pioneers had to deal with the sudden loss of a hero who had provided the words they chanted before taking the ice for every game.

For the Team...
For the Journey...
For the Event...

For the team, the journey would get worse before it got better. By the time it was over the Pioneers had used perseverance, courage, and the inspirational aura provided by their fallen leader to drive themselves to The Event of their lives.

This is not a Cinderella story.

Despite a legacy that will be noted for several fortuitous bounces, an us-against-the-world mentality, and, according to several Pioneers as well as some of Magnuson's former teammates, what seemed at times divine intervention, this is not a "Miracle On Ice" story of vanquishing impossible odds. When the University of Denver won the 2004 NCAA hockey championship, it restored glory to one of the most renowned programs in the history of college hockey. The Pioneers won college hockey's top prize primarily because of their gumption and ability to shrug off adversity. The nerve-wracking adventure that led to Denver's sixth national championship was incalculably inspiring to its fans.

Colorado Governor Bill Owens shows off the L.L. Bean parka and boots he won in a friendly wager over the NCAA championship game with Maine Governor John Elias Baldacci.

Their flair, however, often overshadowed their talent. Just a few days after Denver brought home the trophy, the university hosted an enthusiastic rally at Magness Arena. One of the guest speakers was Colorado Governor Bill Owens, who told the crowd of over 3,100 that he still remembered where he was when the 1980 U.S. Olympic hockey team pulled off the "Miracle on Ice" upset of the Soviet Union. Owens said Coloradoans will always remember where they were for the "Second Miracle on Ice" realized by the Pioneers. Careful observers would have noticed Denver coach George Gwozdecky squirming in his seat behind the governor.

While Governor Owens was on the money on one count - fans who watched DU weather the University of Maine's 6-on-3 opportunity in the final 78 seconds of the championship game surely have the game branded in their memories - Gwozdecky respectfully disagreed with the governor's assessment of the win as miraculous, a claim the coach reiterated at the team's awards banquet weeks later. When Gwozdecky looked down the row of players lined up behind the governor, he didn't see saints who had merely reaped the benefits of good fortune. He saw hard-nosed hockey players who had matured before his eyes, a group that meshed talent and ambition at the perfect time. As a whole, the group was too aloof to work miracles and too driven to write Cinderella stories.

Sure, Denver finished its march to the national championship with a record of 27-12-5, the lowest victory total for a title-winner since 1981. And yes, it was hard to argue that the Pioneers were not a team of destiny after an NCAA tournament run that produced a pair of 1-0 victories and more gut-wrenching moments than a Hollywood thriller. But those footnotes obscure the determination and true team spirit that carried Denver to the program's sixth national championship, its first since 1969.

"You can have certain Cinderella teams, but those Cinderella teams only go so far before they get knocked out either because they don't have the depth, they don't have the skill, or they aren't good enough," a pleasantly weary Gwozdecky said days after his team's 1-0 victory against Maine in the national championship game.

Pioneers head coach George Gwozdecky insists his 2004 national champions were not a "Cinderella team."

"I think the one thing that really discredits our team is when people consider us a Cinderella team. Over the last third of our season, we were one of the hottest teams in the country. Of the teams we played, a great majority of them were ranked in the top 15 in the country. We had a very good first third, we had a miserable middle third, and we had a great last third. This team earned every win they got. This team forced their will on every team they played. They created the bounces we needed, and they felt it really was our time. For anyone to think this was luck would be doing us a disservice, and they would not be understanding of what this team is about."

Indeed, 2004 would prove to be Denver's time. Yet before the Pioneers could hoist the championship trophy they would have to overcome inconsistent play, the shock of Keith Magnuson's sudden death, a surprising roster defection, a rash of injuries, and the discouraging label of "underdog" that greeted them at the Frozen Four in Boston.

This is not a fairy tale. What follows is a tale of grit, perseverance, and determination. The Pioneers weathered more peaks and valleys than they would have encountered on a hike in the mountains that loom over their campus. In the end they learned it was just a bumpy road they had to slog through during The Journey Magnuson prepared them for.

Part I -
For the
Team

For Connor James, the journey began on an airplane thousands of feet above the desolate landscape between Los Angeles and Denver.

James had just completed a training camp for the Los Angeles Kings, which selected him in the ninth round of the 2002 NHL draft. Though drained physically as well as mentally, James was thrilled by the camp experience. It wasn't often James could skate with so many future pros. But now that he was en route to Denver, James put aside his daydreams about a future in the National Hockey League and shifted his thoughts to the present.

In a few months James would begin his final season at the University of Denver. With a Pioneers bio overflowing with impressive stats and commanding performances, he already had plenty to be proud of. A native of Calgary, James chose Denver over Boston University because he felt more comfortable with the coaching staff. He also was intrigued by the plethora of players from Western Canada on the Pioneers' roster. From early on, James had a keen respect for the power of team chemistry.

Surviving the L.A. Kings' camp was hardly a challenge

William R. Sallaz

Senior Connor James went into his final season at DU as a proven Iron Man. James played in all 120 of Denver's games the previous three seasons.

for the durable James. He had never missed a game at Denver, appearing in all 120 games during his first three seasons. James tallied 85 points in 82 games in his sophomore and junior seasons. Heading into his senior year, James was the team's top returning scorer, having produced a career-best 43 points the the prior year.

He was the team's second-leading scorer as a sophomore as well, yet much of his motivation for his upcoming senior year revolved around erasing the memories of the heartbreaking conclusion to Denver's 2001-02 campaign. A plane cruising hundreds of miles an hour wasn't fast enough to allow James to escape the memory of the team's last NCAA tournament experience.

Former Pioneer All-American Wade Dubielewicz (left) and senior Adam Berkhoel (right) formed arguably the best goaltending tandem in the nation for two seasons.

Denver spent most of the last half of James' sophomore season ranked at the top of the national polls. Blessed with a versatile array of skilled forwards, physical defensemen, and the best goaltending tandem in the nation in Wade Dubielewicz and Adam Berkhoel, DU became the first team in 11 years to win the MacNaughton Cup, awarded to the regular season champ of the Western Collegiate Hockey Association, in addition to the league playoffs. They earned the No. 1 seed in the West Region, and in the old 12-team format of the NCAA tournament, the Pioneers only had to win one game in order to make its highly anticipated return to the Frozen Four. James and his classmates - Ryan Caldwell, Adam Berkhoel, Max Bull, Lukas Dora, Greg Keith, and Scott McConnell - would add their names to the school's rich hockey lore.

Unfortunately that one game was against the University of Michigan on the Wolverines' home ice at Yost Arena in Ann Arbor. The Pioneers took a 3-2 lead into the third period but couldn't stop Michigan's momentum once its fans got rolling. The Pioneers suffered a dispiriting 5-3 loss. The failure to achieve their expected return to national glory left an ache in their bones that was renewed after the Pioneers failed to reach the NCAA tournament the next year.

James pondered the ups and downs of his career as his plane streaked toward Colorado. If James and his classmates had one wish for their final season, it would be to finally vanquish the memory of that depressing night in Michigan.

"This year was desperate for us," James said. "As seniors, we didn't want to leave without making up for that. The best thing that happened to us coming in was that we weren't ranked high. That took pressure off a lot of guys. We could sneak in the back door."

James was traveling back to the Mile High City in order to lend a helping hand at University of Denver head coach George Gwozdecky's annual summer camp. Officially, the camp is a time when youngsters cool down from the sweltering summer sun while getting instruction from Gwozdecky, his staff, and his players.

Unofficially, the four-week camp also serves as summer warm-up for the Pioneers. As the team's top returning scorer and one of its assistant captains, James couldn't help but wonder what the coming season would bring as he gazed at the vast horizons outside the plane's windows. He would reunite with teammates both past and present at the camp. Much of the ribbing and trash talking would be aimed at how James' class would fare during the upcoming season.

Of course there would be talk about winning a national championship. They did that every summer, when expectations were at their peak and the wearying grind of the college hockey season was still months away.

"You say it every year," James said. "Certain guys believe it, certain guys don't. We talked about it, but I'm not sure we really talked about it as a possibility. We had smaller goals."

PIONEERS

Director of Athletics and Recreation
Dr. M. Dianne Murphy

August 20, 2004

Mrs. Carol Moore
22 Cherry Hills Park Drive
Cherry Hills Village, CO 80110-7175

Dear Carol:

What a great year for Pioneer Athletics! It certainly was one of the most exciting years in Pioneer history - in fact, it qualifies as our best year yet as a member of NCAA Division I.   The triumphs range from another national hockey championship to a third straight Sun Belt Conference Tournament Title for our women's soccer team. Just as important, we captured our fifth consecutive Sun Belt Conference Graduation Rate Award and our student-athletes earned a 3.266 composite GPA for the 2003-2004 academic year.

Because you are a great fan of the University of Denver athletics program, I want you to have a copy of *Crimson and Gold, The Denver Pioneers Magical Run to the 2004 National Hockey Championship* as a token of our appreciation. I look forward to seeing you soon.

Warmest regards,

M. Dianne Murphy
Director of Athletics and Recreation

Enc.

In an early sign of the unity that eventually would carry the team to the national championship, Denver had its best turnout for the summer session in years. For James and his fellow seniors, the scene at Gwozdecky's camp was reminiscent of the summer workouts the team enjoyed two years earlier, the season when they went on to win the MacNaugton Cup and the Broadmoor Trophy (awarded to WCHA playoff champion).

James talked about achieving small goals, and the first small goal was to survive the exhaustive pace of the four-week camp. A typical day saw the Pioneers up early for sprints before working with the campers throughout the day. At some point each player would find time to hit the weight room.

Napping after the physically taxing day was practically unavoidable. Not because any of the Pioneers had run out of energy, but because they needed to reserve their strength for the scrimmages they held late at night in an empty Magness Arena.

The summer workouts typically attracted many of Denver's active hockey alumni. The session last summer drew, among others, the Minnesota Wild's Antti Laaksonen, Kevin Doell, Greg Barber, and Dubielewicz, who was preparing for his first pro season in the New York Islanders' system. The scrimmages always stoked Denver's competitive fire, whether in games between alumni and current Pioneers or the inherently chippy showdowns between the Americans and Canadians.

Soon, however, summer passed. School began, and before they knew it the Pioneers were back on the ice. There were plenty of questions to answer from the year before, when Denver was a preseason Frozen Four favorite but lost in the first round of the WCHA tournament, finishing 21-14-6. Half of the top six point-producers were gone, including Doell, a 51-point scorer, and WCHA Co-Defensive Player of the Year Aaron MacKenzie. Dubielewicz was gone too, leaving Berkhoel to shoulder the goaltending load by himself.

Denver literally was facing the longest road of any team in the nation. The Pioneers' first game - a date against 14th-ranked Ohio State at the Lefty McFadden tournament in Dayton, Ohio, on October 3 - would also be the first game of the college season, marking the earliest start in the 55-year history of the Pioneers' program.

The early start meant that Gwozdecky and his assistant coaches - Steve Miller, Seth Appert and Chris LaPerle - would be on the ice with the team for only a few practices before departing for Ohio. It also meant that Ryan Caldwell would oversee a handful of captain's practices that had a greater sense of urgency than past seasons.

Not surprisingly, Caldwell would be in the middle of an altercation that would set the groundwork for the feisty attitude that would carry the Pioneers to unimaginable heights.

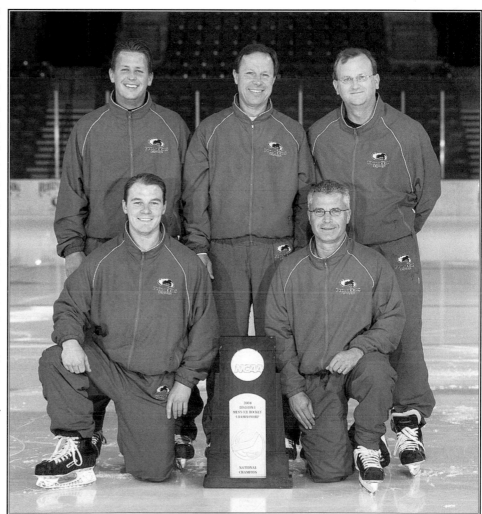

Kevin Ferguson

The 2004 Denver hockey coaching staff: Back Row, L-R, assistant coach Seth Appert, head coach George Gwozdecky and assistant coach Steve Miller; Front Row, L-R, volunteer assistant coach Chris LaPerle and director of hockey operations David Tenzer.

Two of the season's defining moments revolved around Caldwell and his good buddy McConnell, a Colorado Springs native who played sparingly throughout his career yet remained one of the team's most popular players because of his biting wit and constant good spirits. In December Caldwell and McConnell would console each other after becoming the first Pioneers to learn about Magnuson's fatal car accident.

Yet for a few minutes in late September they were doing their best to break each other's jaws.

Tensions boiled over at a captain's practice shortly before the beginning of official workouts. The friends' tempers were simmering throughout the session. After plenty of words and not-so-subtle elbows and hip checks, they finally traded blows along the boards near center ice, where the entire team had a good view.

Though Caldwell suffered the first of two broken fingers that annoyed him throughout the first months of the season, McConnell definitely got the worst of the exchange against the lanky 6-foot-3, 195-pound captain, earning a broken nose that stained his Irish complexion with two black eyes. Even though McConnell had to pass on the team's official Picture Day because of his battered visage, the roommates forgot the incident long before McConnell's injuries healed. Still, the throwdown had a lasting, galvanizing effect on DU's younger players. College hockey was serious business. Not even friends or family were going to impede the Pioneers' quest.

"I think what Ryan and I did was show the underclassmen what we were going to do this year. We still may not go as far as we should, but we're going to fight and earn everything that we get," said McConnell. "It's funny to go back to that point in time and say that a lot of guys thought about this as a point where they had to jump on board or get off the tracks.

"I don't know whether it was the fact that we know each other so well that we knew we should fight, because of the effects it could have, but something clicked at the same time that we should do this. The ripple effects that it had…at the time I thought it was just a little tussle to get everyone going. To see the ripple effects last the entire season, especially toward the end of the season as we kept going and going, I'm glad that we did it. We've never really talked about it. And to hear some of the younger guys choose that point as a get-up-and-go point, it's nice to hear. That's kind of what we did it for."

The Pioneers opened the season in dominant fashion, handing the Buckeyes a 5-2 defeat before Berkhoel pitched a 3-0 shutout against St. Lawrence in the championship game of the Lefty McFadden tournament. Junior forward Jeff Drummond earned the tournament MVP award by posting three goals and an assist in the two wins.

The early-season emergence of Drummond and sophomore Gabe Gauthier proved to be a huge boon to Denver's offense throughout the year. Coming off a 25-point season, Drummond compiled 12 points in the first 10 games, including three consecutive two-point games to begin the year.

Senior captain Ryan Caldwell learned of the untimely death of DU legend Keith Magnuson from teammate and good friend Scott McConnell.

Junior forward Jeff Drummond (right) was named the Most Valuable Player of the Lefty McFadden Invitational after recording three goals and one assist in two Pioneer victories.

Gauthier, a burly center from Buena Park, California, put together an even more impressive start. After serving a one-game suspension against Ohio State and going scoreless against St. Lawrence, Gauthier produced 19 points in the next 12 games. A pair of three-point efforts highlighted the seven multi-point games Gauthier posted during that stretch, a monumental boost of confidence for a highly-touted recruit who managed only 16 points during a disappointing freshman campaign. "I worked a little harder in the summer, but the main thing is I have more confidence in myself," Gauthier said. "I believe in myself, and I know what I can do. Now I'm actually applying it to my game. I'm not focusing on how many points I'm going to get or if I'm going to disappoint people."

After dominating a pair of exhibition games, Denver continued the regular season with a non-conference series against

The emergence of sophomore center Gabe Gauthier (left) was helped by senior linemates Connor James and Lukas Dora.

Northeastern, the Pioneers' first official home games of the year. It was alumni weekend at Denver, a weekend Keith Magnuson did his best not to miss. He made a point of making it this year to celebrate the induction of former teammate Cliff Koroll into the DU Athletics Hall of Fame. Naturally, Magnuson made a lasting impression, first by delivering a fiery pregame speech to the team before the series opener, then by making a surreal appearance at the alumni game the following morning.

"One of my goals with the hockey program has always been to tie the new to the old, the new guys to the tradition," Gwozdecky said. "Having Keith there did that. Plus, I didn't have to make a pregame speech. There was nobody better at giving a fire-up talk than Keith Magnuson, Mr. Pioneer."

The alumni game always is one of the highlights of the weekend, an informal affair typically played on Saturday morning. Koroll arrived just after the game started. Decked out in his suit and tie, Koroll wondered where Magnuson was. Neither of the former Pioneers teammates had skated at Magness Arena since it opened in 1999.

Keith Magnuson (right) and Bruce Hill (center) helped celebrate the University of Denver Athletics Hall of Fame induction of former teammate Cliff Koroll (left) on October 18, 2003.

"Keith was late, for whatever reason. I remember Cliff wondering where he was," Gwozdecky said. "Keith finally shows up in his shirt and tie. Keith looked at Cliff and said, 'You know, we should go skate on this ice. We'll never know if we'll ever get this chance again.' I remember Keith saying that. I'll never forget that."

After some initial resistance, Koroll was swayed, predictably, by Magnuson's boundless enthusiasm. They retreated to the Pioneers' locker room to rummage for skates and gloves. Magnuson laced up the skates he found, slipped off his suit coat, and donned some gloves. The rest of the outfit remained intact when the pair finally hit the ice and joined separate teams.

While Koroll attempted to retain an air of dignity, Magnuson soon began throwing his well-dressed body around the ice. Magnuson, of course, was the last man to leave the ice, savoring his first skate at Magness. His beaming smile and sweat-drenched clothes left their marks on the DU players watching from the sidelines. No one could have fathomed that his first skate at Magness would be his last skate at Magness.

"Me and the other sophomores and freshmen understood the pride of this school coming in," Gauthier said. "We knew this organization had been around awhile. It was built on dreams and tradition. When we saw Cliff and Keith skating in their suits, we all said we wanted to be like that when we grew up. Keith's smile lit up the ice. You could just see how much pride he took in the Denver program."

Magnuson had visited the Pioneers' locker room the night before, inspiring DU to a 5-2 victory in the series opener against Northeastern. One of the phrases the gushing Magnuson reiterated during his speech was for the Pioneers to keep preparing themselves for The Event. They wouldn't know what it is, and they could never guess when they would get there, yet Magnuson promised the Pioneers they would know when they were in The Event when they got there as long as they kept striving throughout what he termed The Journey.

Perhaps only a few DU skaters realized the impact of Magnuson's words as they prepared to hit the ice, but the moment would become the driving inspirational force throughout the season.

The Pioneers completed the expected sweep of Northeastern the following night with a workman-like 6-3 victory that produced a pair of significant milestones. Freshman goalie Glenn Fisher made 22 saves to collect his first career win. Moreover, it was Gwozdecky's 200th win at Denver, making him the only Pioneers coach other than the legendary Murray Armstrong to reach that mark.

Armstrong compiled a 460-215-31 mark in 21 seasons at Denver and was the architect behind the Pioneers' five national championships between 1958 and 1969. It was an honor to become the first coach to ascend anywhere near Armstrong's lofty credentials, yet, in typical fashion, Gwozdecky deflected praise for the accomplishment.

"There are dozens of dozens of people, not even athletes, who have

Freshman goaltender Glenn Fisher's 22 saves in the Pioneers' 6-3 win over Northeastern on October 18, 2003, gave Coach Gwozdecky his 200th career win at Denver. The win was also Fisher's first at DU.

to have things right in order to make this thing go," he said. "Any coach who thinks this is a great personal achievement better take another look. We have been very fortunate to have not only really good players but terrific coaching staffs and terrific auxiliary staffs that allow us to be successful."

Because the early season start put a strain on Gwozdecky's preseason routine, one of the Pioneers' annual rituals had been neglected. Following the sweep against Northeastern, Denver still was without a mission statement for the season. Gwozdecky usually handles that chore himself, working with the entire team to come up with a motivating mantra that will last the entire season. This year Gwozdecky was ready for a change.

"I think over the course of the last few years, my ability to help them develop the kind of mission statement that is going to be meaningful…I just had a feeling the whole process had gone stale," Gwozdecky said. "I was looking for a different person, a different voice."

▲ Rocky Mountain News

DU HOLDS OFF NORTHEASTERN

Saturday, October 18, 2003
By Pat Rooney
SPECIAL TO THE NEWS

The University of Denver hockey team knows it will get plenty of point production from senior Connor James. A question mark surrounding the team has been which players would support James on offense.

One hope was a return to form by senior Lukas Dora, who battled nagging injuries last year after a splendid sophomore season. While it certainly is too early to know if Dora is all the way back, the senior right wing took a few steps in the right direction Friday night against Northeastern.

Dora scored the Pioneers' first goal and provided the key pass on the winning tally to lead DU to a 5-2 victory in the first regular-season home game at Magness Arena. The Pioneers can earn the sweep and collect coach George Gwozdecky's 200th win at DU when the teams complete the non-league series tonight at Magness (7, no television).

"Northeastern should be extremely proud of their effort and performance," said Gwozdecky, who has gone 199-140-26 at DU. "They knocked us off the puck all night long. They won a majority of the battles, whether on faceoffs, along the walls or in front of both nets. We're fortunate that we made a couple of plays when they did break down."

Although Dora missed only two games last season, nagging injuries and inconsistent play dropped his production from 30 points as a sophomore to 19 last season. Those struggles were a memory Friday, as Dora's rebound of a James shot on the power play helped DU overcome a penalty-stained start and a 1-0 deficit.

Jeff Drummond's fourth goal of the season gave the Pioneers a brief 2-1 lead, but a goal by Northeastern's Brian Swiniarski tied the score at 2-2 at the end of the first period. DU took the lead for good less than 5 minutes into the second period when Dora, controlling the puck deep in the right corner, fed Jussi Halme in front of the net to give DU a 3-2 edge.

A short-handed goal by Kevin Ulanski and a power-play goal by freshman Matt Carle, the first of his career, gave the Pioneers (3-0) a cushion down the stretch. Ulanski also had a pair of assists to record the fourth three-point game of his career.

"When I was a sophomore we went all the way to the NCAA playoffs, and I didn't feel like I got too much time off in the off-season," said Dora, a native of the Czech Republic. "I personally need five or six weeks, and that's what I got this year. I got my workouts in the off-season and I feel way better on the ice."

DU senior goaltender Adam Berkhoel had to be sharp early, as a flurry of penalties forced the Pioneers to play most of the first 7 minutes with less than five skaters, including more than a minute when Northeastern enjoyed a 5-on-3 advantage.

But Berkhoel was a stone wall during the final two periods, finishing with 35 saves while notching his 34th career victory. Berkhoel's brightest moment came late in the second period with DU clinging to a 3-2 lead. Berkhoel made a sprawling save against Northeastern's Ray Ortiz, then twisted backward to stymie Ortiz on the rebound.

"Simply put, Adam Berkhoel stole this game for us," Gwozdecky said.

Gwozdecky turned to John Coombe, DU's vice chancellor of intellectual property and events. Coombe was an active supporter of the hockey program and had helped create a leadership program for DU's captains the year before. Coombe's hope was to "empower" the captains as they developed their leadership skills, giving them the freedom to assert authority over teammates who were more like friends than followers. Coombe led leadership seminars with Caldwell and his three assistant captains - Connor James, Max Bull, and Kevin Ulanski. The group took on the task of shaping the mission statement before DU began its WCHA schedule.

"We met four or five times through that leadership group and helped them wrestle through problems," Coombe said. "I think the notion that maybe I could help with the mission statement had its seed in my assistance with the leadership program in general."

Amid their discussions the group realized much of the fiery pregame speech delivered by Magnuson before the Northeastern game was still reverberating in their minds. They quickly settled upon one particular bit of Magnuson's wisdom to be the mission statement.

Captain Ryan Caldwell helped craft the Pioneers' mission statement - For the Team, For the Journey, For the Event - by invoking words Keith Magnuson shared in a pre-game speech against Northeastern.

For the Team….
For the Journey…
For the Event…

"We were looking for something all-encompassing, something that would work for the whole year," Caldwell said. "Something that Keith Magnuson said rang true."

The Pioneers completed their preseason with a 4-0 mark and their mission statement was finally in hand. Denver faced an unenviable assignment for their first WCHA series: A road trip to the always-rocking Mariucci Arena, home of the two-time defending NCAA national champions from the University of Minnesota.

Denver fell 6-2 in its first league game, but responded the following night with a 4-3 win. Berkhoel, who was pulled in the second period the night before, bounced back to record 31 saves. James scored the game-winner in the first minute of the third, continuing an early-season trend that saw the Pioneers play much better on the road than at Magness Arena.

State rival Colorado College was up next, with the home-and-home set further illustrating DU's road prowess. The Pioneers recorded a 5-2 series-opening victory at the Colorado Springs World Arena. Caldwell punctuated the win with DU's most artful goal of the season, patiently catching a rebound of his own shot out of midair with his stick before pushing it past Tiger goaltender Curtis McElhinney.

The win improved DU's record to 6-1. It also established a level of confidence on Olympic-sized ice sheets - the speedy Pioneers had now won two of three on the bigger surfaces - and snapped a three-game losing streak at the World Arena, where the Pioneers would return months later for the NCAA tournament.

Rocky Mountain News

DU QUIETS RIVAL CC

Saturday, November 8, 2003
By Pat Rooney
SPECIAL TO THE NEWS

COLORADO SPRINGS - University of Denver goaltender Adam Berkhoel has heard enough of the derisive chants made by the Colorado College student section that he can successfully reduce the insults to background chatter.

Ryan Caldwell has played in enough big games that his nerves always keep as cool as the ice beneath his skates.

On Friday, Berkhoel and Caldwell provided the type of leadership that always is a requisite in a hostile environment, guiding the Pioneers to a 5-2 win against state rival Colorado College at the Colorado Springs World Arena.

Berkhoel made 25 saves, while Caldwell scored what might be the goal of the year during a three-goal flurry by DU early in the second period.

The Pioneers finished with three power-play goals and a short-handed goal to snap a four-game losing streak against the Tigers, who will aim for a split of the Western Collegiate Hockey Association series tonight at DU's Magness Arena (7, Comcast Cable Channel 21).

"I actually thought for the first 10 minutes our freshmen were our best players," said DU coach George Gwozdecky, who earned only his third win in 21 games against CC in Colorado Springs. "We were very hyper in the first 10 minutes."

CC (5-1-1, 2-1 WCHA) appeared ready to continue its recent domination of the series, netting a goal by Marty Sertich less than 2 minutes into the contest after the Pioneers committed a turnover in their own zone. DU's Gabe Gauthier evened the score at 1-1 with a power-play goal at the 11:47 mark.

DU (6-1, 2-1 WCHA) blew open the match early in the second period, scoring three goals within the first 7 minutes against the reeling Tigers. Lukas Dora put the Pioneers ahead with his second goal of the season, but it was Caldwell's goal less than 3 minutes later that silenced the sold out crowd.

With CC working on a power play, Caldwell tapped the puck out of DU's zone to create a two-on-one opportunity. Caldwell worked the puck up the left wing before launching a shot that was stopped by Tigers goaltender Curtis McElhinney.

McElhinney also stopped Caldwell's rebound, but the puck popped straight up. Caldwell calmly used his stick to collect the puck in midair and push it past McElhinney to give DU a 3-1 lead.

"It reminded me of just fooling around after practice," Caldwell said. "It bounced straight up in the air, and I guess by instinct I just tried to hit it back to myself. It ended up going in for a lucky break."

Jeff Drummond completed the Pioneers' flurry by notching his sixth goal of the year on a rebound of a Kevin Ulanski shot a little more than 2 minutes later.

The Tigers were unable to score on nine power play opportunities, often getting held without a shot against the Pioneers' defense.

To make matters worse for CC, senior captain Colin Stuart suffered a separated shoulder and is expected to miss two to three weeks.

"Half of penalty-killing is goaltending, and Berkhoel was good in that situation," CC coach Scott Owens said.

That, however, remained a distant destination along The Journey. Denver surrendered three third-period goals in a 4-1 loss to Colorado College the next night in the series finale, a loss that began a frustrating stretch of home futility for DU within the WCHA.

Following a tie and a win at Alaska Anchorage, Denver returned to Magness Arena on November 21 to begin a league series against North Dakota. The Pioneers were hoping to use the two games against the nation's top-ranked team as a measure for where they stood against the elite teams. The test ended with discouraging results.

The Fighting Sioux scored 14 goals in a one-sided sweep, recording victories of 8-2 and 6-2. It was the most goals Denver had allowed in a home series in 13 years. Although freshman defenseman Matt Carle was out of the lineup (the Anchorage native suffered a sprained ankle in the first game in front of his hometown crowd the week before), Gwozdecky was disappointed with the effort of his defensemen and his power play units, which managed only one goal in 15 opportunities during the two games.

"If they are going to create so many chances, we want them to work for those chances," he said shortly after the Sioux completed the sweep. "Some of the things we did I'm still

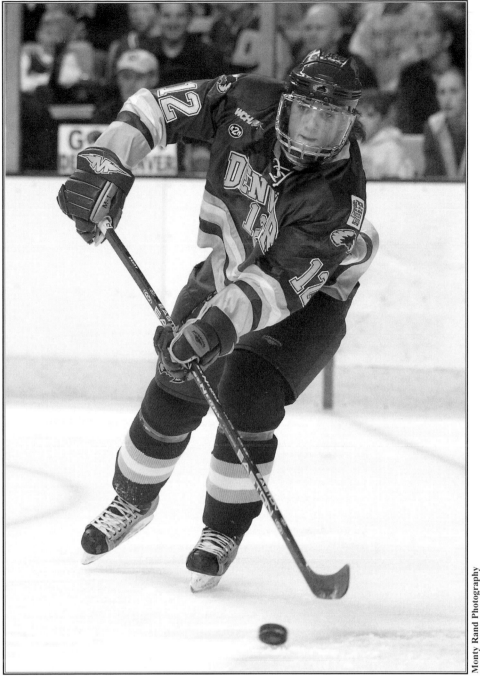

Monty Rand Photography

Freshman defensive standout Matt Carle missed 14 games with an early-season ankle injury and Team USA commitment at the World Junior Championships in Helsinki, Finland.

bewildered at. As a group of six, our defensemen have never played a game as poorly as we did tonight."

It was a telling statement, considering that the core group of defensemen - Caldwell, Carle, Brett Skinner, Matt Laatsch, Jussi Halme, and Nick Larson - would provide some of the most important scoring sparks during the season's stretch run.

Denver cruised through non-league victories against Findlay and Air Force, but the Pioneers' home woes continued when league rival Wisconsin, Gwozdecky's alma mater, brought a nation-leading 10-game unbeaten streak to Magness Arena on December 5. Despite getting third-period goals from Keith and Dora to rally for a 2-2 tie in the opener, the Pioneers allowed the Badgers to continue their streak with a 3-1 win in the finale. DU fell to 0-4-1 at home within the WCHA, and the pair of third-period goals scored by Wisconsin foreshadowed many more turbulent third periods to come.

Rocky Mountain News

PIONEERS SHOW TRUE GRIT IN TIE; DU FACES STREAKING WISCONSIN AGAIN TONIGHT AT MAGNESS

Saturday, December 6, 2003
By Pat Rooney
SPECIAL TO THE NEWS

The third period finally delivered the type of performance University of Denver hockey coach George Gwozdecky had been waiting for, a stretch where the Pioneers' talent and potential was matched by their grit.

The Pioneers earned only one point with their 2-2 tie against Wisconsin on Friday at Magness Arena, but the manner in which DU pulled even should give the team momentum going into the series finale tonight (7, Comcast cable Channel 21).

DU scored two goals in the final 3 minutes, 10 seconds of regulation to erase a two-goal flurry by the Badgers earlier in the period. The Pioneers still have not recorded a win in four Western Collegiate Hockey Association games at home, while Wisconsin extended its NCAA-best unbeaten streak to 11 games.

"We were in second gear in the first period, third gear in the second period, and then finally got it into fourth gear with 6 or 7 minutes left in the game," said Gwozdecky, whose team has not lost to Wisconsin in their past nine games. "We were very fortunate that (goaltender) Adam Berkhoel played as well as he did, otherwise we would be talking about a loss."

Wisconsin (8-3-4, 3-2-4 WCHA) struck first after two scoreless periods, netting a power-play goal by freshman Robbie Earl at the 5-minute, 46-second mark. The Badgers extended their lead to 2-0 on an unassisted goal by sophomore Nick Licari almost 7 minutes later. But senior Greg Keith, who missed the previous three games because of an injury, put the Pioneers on the board with a power-play goal with 3:10 remaining, scoring off an assist from Kevin Ulanski, who also missed the previous two games because of a shoulder injury.

DU (9-4-2, 3-4-2 WCHA) pulled even on the eighth goal of the season by senior Lukas Dora, with 2:10 remaining in regulation. The Pioneers had the best chance to score a winning goal in overtime when a streaking Connor James took a pass from Brett Skinner with about 15 seconds left to play, but James' shot whistled wide of Wisconsin's net.

"It was a great pass from Brett and I gave it all I had," James said. "It just didn't go in, and that's the way it goes sometimes, I guess."

Berkhoel kept DU in the game during what could have been a disastrous first period. The Pioneers were outshot 19-4 during the time frame, but Berkhoel provided several outstanding saves to preserve the scoreless tie. Berkhoel helped kill two Wisconsin power plays during the first period.

Wisconsin outshot the Pioneers 38-33.

"Adam is playing as good as anybody on our team," Gwozdecky said. "He was the wall. He did a terrific job and gave us a chance to get back in the game."

The Pioneers' silver lining throughout what could have been a debilitating start to the season was their ability to perform on the road. It was something the Pioneers leaned on as they prepared for a trip to sixth-ranked St. Cloud State.

"We seem more comfortable on the road," Skinner said at the time. "There really is no explanation for it. Some teams obviously play a lot better at home than on the road. For us it's the other way around. So far we've played some great opponents at home, and maybe that's got us in a bad funk at home. As soon as we find a way to play the same way at home as on the road, I think we'll be rolling."

Denver traveled to St. Cloud with only one win in its previous seven league games. Yet the Pioneers continued their indomitable road show by capturing two wins on the Olympic-sized surface of the Huskies' National Hockey Center. Going into their final WCHA series before the holidays (a return trip to the Land of 10,000 Lakes to face Minnesota State, Mankato) the Pioneers had every reason to focus on the positives of the season's first 11 uneven weeks.

Freshman forward Adrian Veideman displayed versatility by providing valuable minutes along the blue

Versatile freshman Adrian Veideman played 15 games as a defenseman and 29 as a forward. He scored his first career goal against Northeastern on October 17, 2003.

line, while classmate J.D. Corbin began to establish himself as one of the team's speediest wingers. Berkhoel had already posted three shutouts, giving him eight for his career to tie his good friend Dubielewicz for second place on DU's career list. Though limited by his ankle injury, Matt Carle already was showing signs of being a two-way force on the blue line. And Gwozdecky's early-season tinkering with line combinations resulted in one overwhelming success: The top front line of James, Gauthier, and senior right wing Lukas Dora.

"They complement each other," said Gwozdecky. "Connor has terrific speed. Lukas is the kind of guy that goes in there and knocks people off pucks. Gabe is the guy that gets the puck and knows where to distribute it. He's a great, great distributor. Not only that, but he can score. Those three complement each other's strengths."

All the Pioneers had to do was continue their imitation of Road Warriors at ninth-place Minnesota State, Mankato and they would be in third place in the WCHA when they returned to their respective homes for the holidays.

That would have been a remarkable feat for a team that had struggled so thoroughly at home. Little did the Pioneers know that their season would be sundered from all corners within a few days.

Head Coach George Gwozdecky

George Gwozdecky doesn't necessarily believe in fate, luck, or divine intervention. What he does believe in is timing. Timing, he believes, helped everything come together late in the 2003-04 season, which DU capped by winning the school's sixth national championship.

For coaches in any collegiate sport trying to work their way up the ladder, timing is even more imperative. Gwozdecky's first head coaching job in Division I was a five-year tenure with Miami (Ohio). Gwozdecky led the RedHawks to the NCAA tournament in 1992-93 and a 22-16-1 record in 1993-94.

Following that season, though, Gwozdecky was contacted by the University of Denver about its head coaching vacancy. Though off the radar nationally for some time, Denver still boasted a rich history as well as the allure of the Western Collegiate Hockey Association, which Gwozdecky became familiar with as a player at the University of Wisconsin.

Timing led Gwozdecky to check out Denver, but his reaction when he saw DU Arena and the surrounding campus hardly was driven by fate. His reaction was more like *what a dump*.

Gwozdecky and his wife, Bonnie, were comfortable at Miami. The coach's reaction to his new suitors didn't have Bonnie looking up the numbers for moving companies.

"Nothing was really intriguing about Denver," said Gwozdecky. "We had strong ties to Miami and the program. When I came to look at Denver and the program, I was convinced that we had a better program at Miami. At the same time, I had to answer the question of which program could be better in the long run."

Chancellor Daniel L. Ritchie and members of DU's Board of Trustees helped Gwozdecky answer that question. Convinced that Gwozdecky was the man to cultivate the hockey program's role in Ritchie's vision for the entire athletic department, the Chancellor pressed Gwozdecky with the administrative equivalent of a neutral-zone trap in order to bring him to Denver.

Ritchie detailed the perks of Magness Arena and the new surroundings on campus, a project that was finally completed when Magness opened in 1999. Ritchie's enthusiasm was infectious. Gwozdecky became Denver's seventh hockey coach before the 1994-95 season.

"The facility probably was the key component of the program. DU Arena was almost an eyesore," Gwozdecky said. "In order to take the program and make it what Dan's vision was, something had to kick-start it. We needed the facilities to bring the recruits in. This campus has changed so drastically over the years, and the new arena is a big reason why."

Gwozdecky inherited a team that had posted losing records in three of the previous four seasons. The turn-around began in Gwozdecky's first season, as he led the Pioneers to a 25-15-2 mark and a berth in the WCHA Final Five. The following season marked DU's return to the NCAA tournament for the first time since 1986.

In 10 seasons at DU Gwozdecky has compiled a record of 223-152-31, second only to the legendary Murray Armstrong on the Pioneers' all-time win list. The Pioneers have won at least 21 games in seven of 10 seasons under Gwozdecky, and his teams won the WCHA tournament in 1999 and 2002. Gwozdecky has led the Pioneers to five appearances in the NCAA tournament, winning the school's first national championship in 35 years in 2004.

While winning the NCAA tournament was a forgotten thrill for Pioneers fans, it was nothing new to Gwozdecky. DU's 2004 title made Gwozdecky the first person to ever win a national championship as a player (at Wisconsin in 1977), an assistant coach (at Michigan State in 1986), and as a head coach. His keen sense of motivation helped keep the 2004 Pioneers focused when they struggled mightily at midseason, and his decision to let his players relax and have fun at the Frozen Four in Boston was a big reason why they brought the championship trophy back to Denver.

"I've had coaches in championship games before that were worried about getting enough rest and focused on the game 24-7," sophomore center Gabe Gauthier said. "That would only get us nervous. With the approach of relaxing and having fun in Boston, we were ready to go. When we were down earlier in the year he told us we still controlled our own destiny. That all transferred to the way we played."

George, Adrienne and Bonnie Gwozdecky

Part II - For the Journey

George Gwozdecky doesn't get to enjoy many quiet moments during the heart of the hockey season. Almost every minute is consumed by his job, whether he's busy game-planning for the Pioneers' upcoming opponent, outlining practice schedules, or dealing with the headaches that come with juggling the vastly different temperaments of over two dozen college hockey players.

Once autumn and winter roll around Gwozdecky doesn't have much time to spend with his wife, Bonnie, and their daughter, Adrienne.

The University of Denver's coach was savoring one of those unusual moments of solitude on the night of December 15, 2003. Gwozdecky had every reason to feel peaceful in his quiet home. The Pioneers had just swept sixth-ranked St. Cloud State on the road. Denver had a good chance of ending the first half of its conference schedule in the top three, despite its shortcomings at home. The team was relatively healthy, and following that week's series at Minnesota State, Mankato, DU's skaters would head home for the holidays, providing a timely break in the team's demanding schedule.

Gwozdecky's moment of peace was jarred by a phone call shortly after Adrienne was put to bed. On the line was Emory Sampson, a Pioneers winger in the early 1960's and the husband of Denver's faculty athletics representative, Dr. Nancy Sampson. He was calling to inform Gwozdecky of some unfathomable news. Keith Magnuson had died hours earlier in a car accident outside Toronto. Mr. Pioneer was gone.

"It popped in my mind that there is no way an ordinary traffic accident would kill a guy like Keith. He's too tough," Gwozdecky said. "I thought maybe they had made a mistake. Maybe he was recovering, that they thought he was going to pass away but he'll actually be OK. Something as simple as a car accident is not going to be the way Keith is going to leave this world."

But a car accident did take Magnuson from this world, on a road north of Toronto. The 56-year old Magnuson, who was returning from the funeral of former NHL star Keith McCreary, was riding in the passenger seat of a car driven by former Toronto Maple Leafs captain Rod Ramage. Ramage, who survived the crash,

Keith Magnuson was killed in a tragic car accident outside of Toronto on December 15, 2003. The Pioneers honored Magnuson with an on-ice tribute prior to their contest against Alaska Anchorage on January 24, 2004.

Crimson & Gold: The Denver Pioneers' Magical Run to the 2004 National Championship ═══════ **23**

lost control of the vehicle and swerved across the centerline, colliding head-on with an SUV. Magnuson was pronounced dead at the scene.

Magnuson was named to the 75th anniversary team of the Chicago Blackhawks in 2001. He played in two NHL All-Star games and coached the Blackhawks for nearly two seasons, yet Magnuson always maintained that his best hockey memories were forged at the University of Denver. He led DU to national championships in 1968 and 1969, amassing 16 goals and 59 assists in three seasons. His impact on the college game was monumental; Magnuson was named to the first team of the *Hockey News'* WCHA 50th anniversary squad as well as the NCAA's 50th anniversary team.

While he remained close to the Blackhawks organization and was active in the NHL Alumni Association, Magnuson never strayed far from the Pioneers' program. His visit to Denver's locker room two months earlier was routine for Magnuson, who also usually drove from his home in suburban Chicago to Madison, Wisconsin, whenever the Pioneers were visiting the Wisconsin Badgers.

Simply put, Magnuson loved the University of Denver. Suddenly the inspiration for the Pioneers' newly-adopted mission statement was gone.

"I remember him saying so many times that he

William R. Sallaz

Head coach George Gwozdecky was shocked to hear "Mr. Pioneer" Keith Magnuson died in a car accident.

owed all he had to DU and Murray Armstrong," Gwozdecky said. "He would say, 'I'm just a dumb kid from Saskatchewan and all of the sudden DU opened so many doors for me.' He said he'd forever be indebted to Coach Murray and DU hockey."

Magnuson's shocking death abruptly extinguished the momentum the Pioneers gained with their sweep at St. Cloud State the previous weekend and sent them grieving into their first truly tumultuous week of the season.

The tempest began when sophomore defenseman Scott Drewicki made a surprising decision to quit the team a few days after Magnuson's death. Drewicki recorded two assists in 25 games as a freshman, and though he still may have been stinging by a suspension that kept him on the sideline for much of the first part of the season, the timing of Drewicki's decision remained curious. Drewicki had played in two of the previous three games, and since it was no secret the Pioneers had health and manpower issues on the blue line, Drewicki likely would have had more than enough ice time in the approaching weeks to stake his claim to the role of sixth defenseman.

"I think Scott had done a pretty good job during his suspension of handling things he needed to handle," Gwozdecky said. "It was his feeling that he wanted to be able to play more."

The loss of Drewicki (he eventually transferred to Merrimack) forced Gwozdecky to juggle his defensive rotation as the Pioneers prepared for a visit to Minnesota State, Mankato to meet the Mavericks. It was the only WCHA series taking place that weekend as well as DU's final league series for three weeks.

Without Drewicki, Denver's blueliners limped into Mankato, Minnesota. Matt Carle, who had missed eight of the past nine games because of a sprained ankle, joined Team USA for the World Junior Championships in

Finland and was not expected to return to Denver until the second week of January. Nick Larson was gritting his way through knee and ankle problems, while fellow junior Matt Laatsch still was not fully recovered from a rib injury that kept him out of the Wisconsin series. Captain Caldwell was beginning to feel the first painful flares of a knee injury that would plague him the rest of the season.

The Pioneers arrived in Mankato with grieving hearts and groaning defensemen. Because of the holiday calendar, Denver wasn't going to have much of a holiday break. No bye weeks were scheduled until the end of January. Yet the Pioneers remained optimistic about the weekend's opportunity. Earning three points against the ninth-place Mavericks would push Denver into third place in the WCHA with a home-heavy league slate looming in January. Denver recorded a sweep during their visit to Mankato two years earlier and went into the series with a road record of 8-1-1. The Pioneers were hoping for inspiration from their departed Denver hockey brother, but Magnuson apparently hadn't yet adjusted to his new role of spiritual leader.

Sporting new decals on their helmets in honor of Magnuson, the Pioneers began the series by once again behaving like rude guests. The first career goal by freshman Ryan Helgason, followed by a score from Caldwell, gave DU a 2-0 lead at the end of the first period.

Denver was in line to notch its fifth consecutive road win, but the dark cloud that had been hovering over the team in recent days suddenly descended with devastating consequences. After getting rocked by Magnuson's death and a teammate's defection, the Pioneers started carrying their already hurting defensemen from the ice.

Jussi Halme, a junior from Finland, was injured on the first shift of the game when he unselfishly hit the ice to block a Mavericks shot. Thanks to the awkward angle, the screaming slap shot managed to smack Halme below the lip of his mask. He suffered a broken jaw that kept him out of the lineup for three weeks. Caldwell absorbed a menacing hit early in the game, and while the captain stubbornly refused to leave the ice, it was obvious his game was off.

"He wasn't playing well. Very careless and reckless," Gwozdecky said. "His decisions with the puck and his decisions who to step up on, who to check, who to defend…it was like he was a freshman again. I remember telling Seth (assistant coach Seth Appert) we had to limit his playing time in the third period until he got his game back."

Junior defenseman Jussi Halme suffered a broken jaw on the first shift of Denver's December 19 contest at Minnesota State, Mankato. Halme would miss six games before returning to the lineup on January 10.

William R. Sallaz

Caldwell, who was diagnosed with a concussion afterward, couldn't shake the fog. A 19-shot second period by the Mavericks resulted in three goals, but the Pioneers regained the lead on goals by Luke Fulghum and Connor James early in the third period. When Minnesota State, Mankato pulled goalie Jon Volp in the final minute, Gwozdecky had forwards Adrian Veideman, Greg Keith, and Max Bull in the defensive rotation. In the final seconds a dizzy Caldwell whiffed on an attempted check in the corner, forcing the rest of DU's outmanned defenders to scramble. Amid the confusion, the Mavericks were able to push the tying goal past Berkhoel with 1.2 seconds remaining, forcing the Pioneers to settle for a draw.

It was a debilitating if not disastrous result, given the situation. Carle was gone, Halme and Caldwell had been sent to the shelf, and Drewicki was off the team. On Saturday the Pioneers briefly lost their coach, as Gwozdecky flew to Chicago to attend Magnuson's funeral in suburban Lake Forest, Illinois. Yet if the shorthanded Pioneers were wallowing in misery, if they were stewing about the point they lost in the span of a heartbeat, it didn't show at the beginning of a painfully forgettable series finale.

Playing without Halme and Caldwell, the Pioneers, in fact, began by expunging their pent-up emotions upon the Mavericks. Four first-period points by Gabe Gauthier (two goals, two assists) highlighted Denver's six-goal frame. The Pioneers chased Volp with three goals in a span of 2:15, then chased his replacement, Kyle Nixon, on a goal by Jeff Drummond midway through the second period.

Denver led 7-1 with 10 minutes remaining in the second period and barely flinched when the Mavericks cut the lead to 7-2 moments later.

Then a fairly innocuous slashing penalty on Lukas Dora began a tailspin that would have lasting ramifications and prove tougher to shake than a nasty head cold.

Just eight seconds after Dora

Gabe Gauthier emerged as one of DU's top offensive forces in 2003-04. Gauthier's most prolific game came at Minnesota State, Mankato on December 20, 2003, when he recorded his first career four-point game with two goals and two assists, all in the first period.

was sent to the box, Laatsch was whistled for checking from behind. Referee Don Adam deemed Laatsch's hit was delivered with intent to injure and penalized the junior defenseman with a game misconduct. Yet another defenseman was gone, and the five-minute major also gave the Mavericks a 5-on-3 advantage.

Minnesota State, Mankato used the extended power play to score twice within eight seconds, adding a third goal 31 seconds later that whipped the 3,650 fans at the Midwest Wireless Civic Center into a frenzy. Assistant coach Steve Miller, filling in for Gwozdecky, pondered his limited options. Ideally, Miller says, he would have pulled Berkhoel for the remainder of the second period, allowing the senior to regroup for the third. But freshman goalie Glenn Fisher was unavailable because of an ankle injury, and with the clock still ticking on Laatsch's five-minute major, Miller couldn't make a move. As tired forwards took extra shifts along the blue

Kevin Ferguson

While subbing for George Gwozdecky, assistant coach Steve Miller suffered through a roller coaster of emotions as an injury-ravaged group of DU defenseman squandered a 7-1 lead at Minnesota State.

line, Miller could only watch as the Mavericks took over.

"They scored to make it 7-3 and (assistant coach) Seth Appert called down to take a timeout," Miller said. "There was still the major on the ice and I didn't even talk to them. We just needed to get refocused. But the momentum was gone. At that point it was anybody's game, and we hardly had any defensemen."

The reeling Pioneers couldn't recover. The Mavericks scored a short-handed goal to cut DU's lead to one, then scored the tying and game-winning goals within 62 seconds late in the third period. Denver limped into its brief holiday recess in fifth-place in the WCHA and disgusted by the fact it had earned only one point in two easily winnable games.

Gwozdecky, who missed his original flight back to Mankato from Chicago, couldn't quite process the boggling phone report he received from Miller later that evening.

"Steve wears his emotions on his sleeve. You know exactly how he's feeling from the first word he says. And I know he's down," Gwozdecky said. "He said we had a 7-1 lead. I'm thinking we went into overtime and tied, or we let a big lead go and won 7-6 or 8-5. And he said we lost 8-7. I wanted to say 'You're kidding,' but I knew it was serious."

Gwozdecky got back to Mankato in time to release the dejected team for the holidays, though they would have to return to Denver in less than a week to prepare for the 12th annual Wells Fargo Denver Cup. The Cup games against Niagara and Nebraska-Omaha would be the first of four consecutive non-league games, allowing the Pioneers to lick their wounds outside the brutal WCHA slate.

Before the puck dropped for Denver's first home game following Magnuson's death, fans were treated to a video tribute to the fallen star on the JumboTron at Magness Arena. The Pioneers also unveiled a patch on their jerseys that read "K2M" and officially dedicated the rest of the season to Magnuson.

Though sluggish from a whirlwind week of travel, the Pioneers opened the Denver Cup with a 3-2 win against Niagara. Helgason, Keith, and Jon Foster each scored in the second period while Fisher turned in his best performance of the year, making 36 saves and posting his first career assist to lead the win. The next night Denver won its fourth consecutive Denver Cup and 10th overall with a 6-3 win against Nebraska-Omaha. Connor James was named tournament MVP after recording three assists in the two games. He was joined on the all-tournament team by Fisher, Caldwell, and Lukas Dora, who led the win against Omaha with a goal and two assists.

Denver coasted through two more non-conference games the following week against St. Lawrence and Wayne State. Berkhoel blanked St. Lawrence for the second time that year, giving him nine career shutouts to break a tie with Wade Dubielewicz for second place on the Pioneers' all-time shutouts list.

"Everybody is very happy for Adam," Gwozdecky said. "Everybody who is on this team will have a chance to remember sometime down the road that they were part of this record-breaking opportunity that Adam Berkhoel had. Good things happen to good people, and there's no better people than Adam Berkhoel."

Rocky Mountain News

SAINTS CAN'T MARCH PAST DENVER GOALIE

Saturday, January 3, 2004
By Pat Rooney
SPECIAL TO THE NEWS

St. Lawrence hockey coach Joe Marsh might be wondering just how long it will take his team to score a goal against Adam Berkhoel. Apparently 2 hours of hockey wasn't enough time for the Saints to solve the University of Denver's senior goaltender.

Berkhoel shut out the Saints for the second time this season Friday night, leading the Pioneers to a 2-0 victory at Magness Arena. It was the fourth shutout of the season for Berkhoel, who recorded a 3-0 win against St. Lawrence on Oct. 4.

The performance also was the ninth shutout of Berkhoel's career, which broke a tie with former teammate Wade Dubielewicz for second place on DU's career-shutout list. Gerry Powers, who manned the pipes for the Pioneers' national championship seasons of 1968 and 1969, is at the top of the list with 13.

Luke Fulghum and Jeff Drummond provided the goals for DU, scoring in the first and second periods, respectively. Both players scored goals against the Saints earlier this season.

"To pass (Dubielewicz) is a pretty big deal, said Berkhoel, who made 28 saves. "We were chatting (Thursday) night, and we were going to call him again (Friday). I have to give him a call and see what he has to say. Defensively, we didn't give them a whole lot. I saw everything. When I can see shots and (the defense) is letting me see things, it is an easy game for me."

Berkhoel, who also moved into a tie for ninth place on DU's career-wins list, helped kill four St. Lawrence power plays to offset an impressive performance by Saints goalie Mike McKenna. DU outshot St. Lawrence 35-28, but could only push two of those shots past McKenna.

McKenna kept his net clean during four power-play chances, including a 5-minute game misconduct on Saints' leading scorer T.J. Trevelyan at the end of the first period. Trevelyan came into the game with 20 points but was unavailable for the final two periods.

"I thought it was a real goaltender battle," DU coach George Gwozdecky said. "I thought McKenna played extremely well. There were times we didn't finish around the net, but at other times we made plays - McKenna did a great job of keeping them close."

Fulghum put DU on the board 13 minutes, 22 seconds into the game with his eighth goal of the season, beating McKenna off an assist from Lukas Dora. Drummond gave the Pioneers a two-goal cushion late in the second period with his ninth goal of the year, slipping the puck past McKenna on a rebound of his own shot.

Senior Connor James set up Drummond's goal with his 18th assist, extending his scoring streak to six games.

"Connor made a great play," Drummond said. "The rebound kicked right back out, and I just tried to get my stick on it. It definitely was a good goal for us because it gave us some momentum going into the third period."

DU (14-6-3), which improved to 9-0 in games outside the Western Collegiate Hockey Association, will look to keep its perfect nonleague record intact tonight against Wayne State (7, no television). St. Lawrence (6-11-3) travels to Colorado College to face the Tigers at the Colorado Springs World Arena.

▓Rocky Mountain News

PIONEERS ICE DENVER CUP; MVP JAMES LEADS DU IN WIN AGAINST NEBRASKA-OMAHA

Monday, December 29, 2003
By Pat Rooney
SPECIAL TO THE NEWS

Connor James was supposed to provide the offensive backbone for the University of Denver hockey team this season.

And while James certainly was not invisible at the outset of the season - he posted five points in the Pioneers' first eight games - he still did not enjoy the type of production that was expected from a player who compiled 85 points in 82 games during the previous two seasons.

But as a new year is set to begin, it looks as if the old James again is wrecking havoc with opposing defenses. James recorded two assists during a three-goal first period Sunday to help lead DU to a 6-3 victory against Nebraska-Omaha in the final of the Wells Fargo Denver Cup at Magness Arena.

James, who notched an assist during the Pioneers' win against Niagara on Saturday, led the all-tournament team as its most valuable player. It was the second consecutive appearance for James on the all-tournament team, which included teammates Lukas Dora, Ryan Caldwell and Glenn Fisher.

The victory marked the 10th time in 12 years the Pioneers have won the championship of their holiday tournament. Niagara finished in third place with a 2-1 win against Yale on Sunday afternoon.

"I'd like to think that, being an assistant captain and a senior, the pressure wouldn't get to me. But I think it did a little," said James, who has posted seven points during his current five-game scoring streak. "When things don't go the way you want, you start doing things you normally wouldn't do. But time always tells. Hockey players go through highs and lows and, hopefully, the lows are gone."

Dora added a goal and two assists, while Ted O'Leary recorded the first multiple-point game of his career with two assists to help take the pressure off DU's injury-riddled defensive corps. Senior goalie Adam Berkhoel made 23 saves to post the 42nd win of his career, which moved him into a tie for 10th place on DU's all-time wins list.

"I'm feeling more confident as I've been getting in the games more," said O'Leary, a sophomore from Arvada. "With all three assists this weekend, all I had to do was put (the puck) in a good area. But it felt great to get some points and play some more."

Freshman Ryan Helgason put eighth-ranked DU on the board less than 3 minutes into the contest with his third goal this season, converting a rebound of a shot by O'Leary. James earned assists on subsequent goals by Gabe Gauthier and Kevin Ulanski that gave the Pioneers a 3-0 lead.

The Mavericks scored twice late in the first period to trim the Pioneers' lead to 3-2 entering the second. But a power-play goal by Dora, followed by the first goal this season by senior Max Bull, 33 seconds later, gave DU a 5-2 edge.

Luke Fulghum capped the scoring for DU (13-6-3), scoring his seventh goal this season, early in the third, off assists by Jeff Drummond and Dora.

"I wouldn't say (Saturday) was a great effort, but (Sunday) we took advantage of some of our opponents' weaknesses," DU coach George Gwozdecky said. "I thought the third period was as good a managed period that we have had all year."

The fifth-ranked Pioneers continued their eight-game homestand with a 4-2 victory against Wayne State, netting two goals in each of the final two periods to give Fisher his second consecutive win. Despite playing without Carle and Halme, DU managed to record wins in each of its four games following the disaster in Mankato. Denver completed its non-conference schedule with a record of 10-0, but they were about to resume WCHA play with a home series against Minnesota-Duluth, which had won three of four games against Denver the year before.

Duluth also featured a pack of top-flight offensive talents, led by Junior Lessard, that could rival any attack in the nation. The Pioneers were 0-4-1 at home in league play, and some around the program believed the four straight wins against the lesser-quality non-conference opponents had failed to erase the nightmare of the Mankato series.

"I told the guys to not let that bother us for our next games at the Denver Cup. And it didn't," Miller said. "Unfortunately it affected us against Duluth. I think we were still doubting ourselves."

Gwozdecky agreed, sensing the downtrodden spirit of his team.

"That game at Mankato took something out of us," he said. "We knew we were better than the four teams we had to play in those non-conference games. Getting back into the conference was going to be a challenge. Tougher games, games that meant more, games that required us to find our soul. That damn game at Mankato threw us for a loop that we didn't recover from for weeks."

Though Halme remained on the sidelines with a broken jaw, a healthy Carle made a triumphant return to the lineup after helping the United States to its first gold medal at the World Junior Championships. His steadying presence on the blue line, however, was not enough to change DU's fortunes at home. Denver dominated all aspects of the opener against Duluth except the scoreboard, falling 1-0 despite creating ample scoring opportunities. James missed a breakaway, Denver failed in nine power play opportunities, and the Pioneers outshot the Bulldogs 32-19, yet they couldn't get by Duluth goaltender Isaac Reichmuth.

University of Minnesota-Duluth Media Relations

Minnesota-Duluth's Junior Lessard led the Bulldogs to a sweep of the Pioneers at Magness Arena in January. Lessard finished the season with the most points in the nation and won the Hobey Baker Award.

Denver, still mired in fifth-place in the WCHA, needed a win in the finale to stay within one point of fourth-place Duluth. The game was so important that the Pioneers' walking wounded felt compelled to make a comeback. Halme made his first appearance in three weeks after having the wires removed from his injured jaw only days earlier. Gauthier (shoulder) and Laatsch (knee) both missed the opener because of mild injuries but donned their skates for the finale, giving Denver a full lineup for the first time since early November.

The team's confidence, however, remained critically low, and the Pioneers replayed a scene that was becoming depressingly familiar to their fans.

Denver answered an early Duluth goal with scores by freshman J. D. Corbin and James, giving DU a 2-1 lead at the end of the first period. The Bulldogs sandwiched goals around a power play goal by junior Kevin Ulanski during the second period, sending the teams into the final period in a 3-3 tie.

WCHA opponents were making it impossible for DU to chase away its third period blues, and the Bulldogs were no exception. Two rapid-fire Duluth goals midway through the frame chased Berkhoel and set up a 6-3 Pioneers loss.

Bruised but finally intact, Denver trudged into its first bye week since late October. Their home record within the league dipped to 0-6-1, and the sweep by Duluth dropped DU from fifth to 10th in the national polls. The only bright spot was that they finally had a chance to take a deep breath and let their wounds heal. A promising proposition, since three of the Pioneers final six regular-season series would be against the bottom three teams in the WCHA.

"It's times like this when you really have to suck it up," Gwozdecky said. "You have to move on, and you have to work even harder in all areas of your student-athlete life."

The bye week left Denver tied for sixth in the WCHA with Alaska Anchorage, its opponent the next weekend at Magness Arena. DU had its freshest legs in months as well as a 10-game unbeaten streak against the Seawolves. The stars were aligned for Denver to post its first home WCHA win of the season.

With Gwozdecky calling a victory in the opener "absolutely imperative," Denver produced

Speedy freshman J.D. Corbin developed a knack for creating scoring chances. He finished his rookie campaign with three goals and six assists.

William R. Sallaz

another sizable advantage in shots (39-26) but watched Anchorage take a 1-0 lead into the third period. Dora finally tied the game on a power play goal with 6:50 remaining, sending the game into overtime. James took advantage of another power play opportunity early in the extra session, tapping home a rebound of a deflected Gauthier shot for his eighth goal of the season. Denver increased its unbeaten streak against Anchorage to 11 and finally collected its elusive first home win within the WCHA.

"This gives the guys a lot of confidence, especially to get the win at home. It means a lot," James said. "It could have gone either way, but we got a bounce at the end that we buried."

The Pioneers were poised to record their first home sweep of a WCHA team, but they had yet to find a good luck charm that could negate the curse of the third period. For once, a rather sizable group of college guys were absolutely dreading Saturday nights.

Rocky Mountain News

JAMES STICKS WITH IT, ENDS DU'S HOME HEX

Saturday, January 24, 2004
By Pat Rooney
SPECIAL TO THE NEWS

A s one of the alternate captains for the University of Denver hockey team, Connor James does not hesitate to take it upon himself to find unorthodox ways to break bad streaks when his team is in a rut.

On Thursday, a little more than 24 hours before the opening of a key league series against Alaska-Anchorage, James gave his stick a fresh coat of black paint in hopes of snapping his personal scoring drought.

On Friday, James' hex-breaking ritual paid dividends. The senior forward used his freshly charmed stick to record an assist late in regulation and score the winning goal in overtime, leading the Pioneers to 2-1 victory at Magness Arena. The win was DU's first at home in league play this season and breaks a tie with the Seawolves in the Western Collegiate Hockey Association standings.

The Pioneers will hold sole possession of sixth place when the teams meet tonight in the series finale (7, no television).

"It's nice to win one at home, especially against this team," James said. "This team is not the Anchorage of the past. They are a top-notch hockey team. It could have gone the other way, but we got the bounce at the end."

Freshman Charlie Kronschnabel gave Anchorage an early lead with a power-play goal less than 8 minutes into the contest. The 1-0 score held until the third period, despite a DU effort that produced a 39-26 advantage in shots.

James' contribution to the tying goal was slightly accidental. With DU working on the power play, James partially whiffed on a pass across the crease to Lukas Dora. But the Anchorage defense went reeling from James' heavy stick action as if it was a changeup, and Dora buried his 10th goal of the season with 6 minutes, 50 seconds remaining in regulation.

James' winner, which came on the power play as well, was his eighth goal of the season. Gabe Gauthier began the scoring play with a blast from the point that deflected off Dora's stick before reaching Anchorage goalkeeper Chris King.

James collected the rebound and put home the winner with 2:58 remaining. The assists by James and Gauthier were their team-leading 20th assists of the season.

"In our recent games we lost our composure," DU goalkeeper Adam Berkhoel said. "(Friday night) we really kept sticking with it. We were down 1-0, but we were really playing our (tails) off. We finally got that monkey off our backs."

Despite extending its undefeated streak against the Seawolves to 11 games, DU suffered an early setback when captain Ryan Caldwell absorbed a hard check from Anchorage's Curtis Glencross late in the first period. Caldwell left the game because of a knee injury and did not return. He is not expected to be ready for tonight.

"This was a really challenging, difficult game for us," DU coach George Gwozdecky said. "Chris King played really well in goal for (Anchorage). We made a couple real key adjustments to our forward lines going into the third period, especially on the power play, and we are really glad we did. It was great to see James come back on two huge goals when a week ago he couldn't buy a goal."

Head coach Gwozdecky and his Pioneers looked nothing like a potential national champion at the end of January, when they owned a 1-7-1 mark at home within the WCHA.

First-period goals by Keith and Veideman staked the Pioneers to the lead, which Gauthier extended to 3-1 with a power play goal midway through the second period. Denver was 20 minutes from taking a commanding lead over the Seawolves in the WCHA standings when the wheels fell off with even more disturbing results than the game at Mankato or the loss to Duluth two weeks earlier.

Alaska Anchorage sophomore Curtis Glencross, who would leave school to sign a free agent contract with the Anaheim Mighty Ducks following the season, cut DU's lead to 3-2 less than two minutes into the third period. Improbably, the Pioneers surrendered the first goals of the season for Vladimir Novak and Nick Lowe later in the frame. The two Anchorage skaters found the net within 99 seconds of each other, and once Lowe added another goal on an empty-netter in the final minute, the Seawolves were celebrating a 5-3 win.

DU was left to deal with another debilitating home loss. Denver director of athletics Dr. M. Dianne Murphy had to watch the home fans grow increasingly irritated at Magness Arena. She realized the fans felt much like she did; the losses themselves weren't as maddening as was the way the team was playing.

"I'm not going to say I wasn't disappointed, because I was. We all were. The players were disappointed, the coaches were disappointed, because we knew we had a better team. We had better talent than how we were playing," Murphy said. "My biggest disappointment is that we weren't living up to our potential, and we weren't doing smart things on the ice. That part is what was disappointing."

The failure against Alaska Anchorage marked the sixth time Denver allowed at least three third-period goals (not including a three-goal third by the University of British Columbia during an exhibition game), leaving the Pioneers to simmer over yet another lost opportunity. As he did throughout his team's struggles, Gwozdecky tried to latch on to the positives even as the Pioneers slipped further down the WCHA standings.

"It's very obvious I think we're all disappointed. But I don't look at that third period against Anchorage as much as I look at those first two periods," he said. "We worked hard. We had a great start. We created a lot of good chances. We really controlled the game in every aspect except on the scoreboard. For whatever reason, we struggled to score. The big factor in the game was our inability to put them away when we had chances. We played really, really well in the first two periods."

Denver outshot Anchorage by a mind-boggling 50-29 in the finale, the first time in over two years that DU posted 50 shots in a game. Yet the Pioneers managed only 12 shots in the third period after producing 38 in the first 40 minutes. Berkhoel surrendered three goals on nine shots in the final frame.

The entire Pioneers program fell into a frustratingly dark haze. Off the ice, DU's administration was alarmed by reports of alleged misbehavior on and around campus by the players. Every single accusation proved to be unfounded, but in light of the various scandals dominating the headlines throughout Colorado, many players were subjected to lengthy meetings with Gwozdecky and associate athletics director Ron Grahame, a former DU goaltender who helped lead the Pioneers to the national championship game in 1973.

Though the Pioneers were exonerated, the incidents only added to the disappointment and frustration they were experiencing on the ice.

"I remember telling assistant coaches Seth Appert and Steve Miller that I don't recall a more challenging time in my coaching career as that time period was," Gwozdecky said. "Having to try to figure out what this team needs to do to get through this and turn things around…on the outside you're trying to show the guys there's nothing wrong, that we're confident in you guys, and we'll make it no problem. And yet up here," Gwozdecky taps his forehead, "I'm thinking we've got to figure something out.

"Through the many meetings that we had as a staff, that we had with the team, that we had with others, like Ron Grahame, to get feedback from them, I think we finally started to get some ideas that I think we used to help us. Or at least were factors in getting our team to get their confidence back and make us more competitive and successful."

Gwozdecky, his staff, and Denver's seven seniors soon would help the team piece together its shattered confidence. But not before the Pioneers endured a little more misery - misery that would push them to their breaking point - during a landmark road trip to Grand Forks, North Dakota.

The guidance of many of DU's support staff, including associate athletics director and former DU goaltender Ron Grahame (right), helped nurture the leadership skills of captain Ryan Caldwell (left) and his fellow seniors.

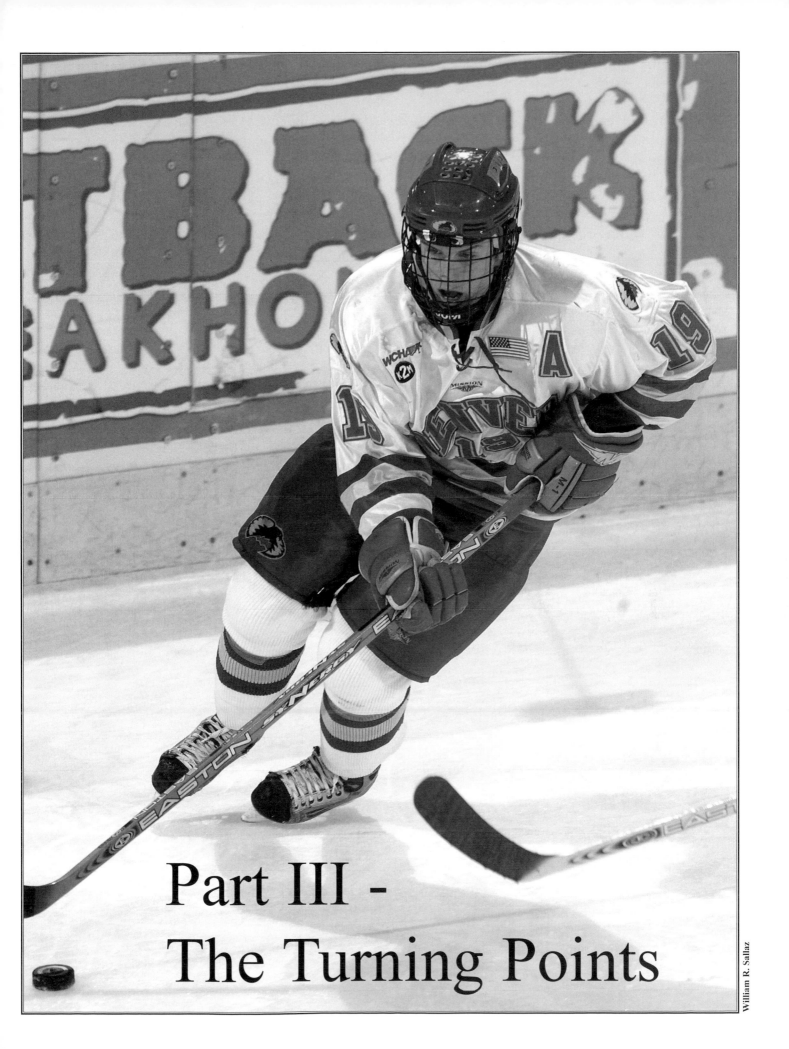

Part III -
The Turning Points

The reeling Pioneers were greeted by record low temperatures upon their arrival in Grand Forks, North Dakota, where the winter winds were punishing the vast northern flatlands. The gusts were brutal, their chill a fitting complement to the team's foul mood. Though violently loud, the gales went unnoticed by the Pioneers, drowned out by the gurgling sound of their season spiraling down the drain.

Denver had just completed a homestand with consecutive Saturday night third-period meltdowns against Minnesota-Duluth and Alaska Anchorage. The Pioneers had won only one of their past six league games to fall into a tie for seventh place in the WCHA. To top it off, Denver faced the daunting challenge of trying to begin its recovery at North Dakota's wild Engelstad Arena, where a pair of overtime losses eliminated them from the WCHA playoffs a year earlier. While Denver had proven to be a tough road team, the Pioneers were completely punchless against North Dakota during two lopsided home losses in November. Like sharks circling a wounded prey, the top-ranked Fighting Sioux wasted little time inflicting more carnage upon the embattled Pioneers in the January 30 series opener.

North Dakota freshman Brady Murray, the son of Los Angeles Kings coach Andy Murray (who, coincidentally, coached Ryan Caldwell and Max Bull at Shattuck-St. Mary's prep school in Minnesota), put Denver in a hole while the fans were still settling into their seats, scoring two goals in a span of 1:47 during the opening minutes. Brandon Bochenski, one of the Fighting Sioux's two Hobey Baker candidates, added a power play goal minutes later, giving North Dakota a 3-0 edge and chasing Adam Berkhoel before the game was 11 minutes old.

Once North Dakota's feeding frenzy ended, DU found itself on the wrong end of a demeaning 6-1 decision. The Pioneers had now been outscored 20-5 in three games against the Fighting Sioux. After playing so well on the road to that point, the latest setback further diminished the team's confidence that they could compete with the best teams in the nation.

Denver officially hit rock bottom. The season was slipping out of control. The Pioneers couldn't hold a lead at home, and now apparently their road magic was gone, too. The Journey, for all practical purposes, would end

North Dakota's Brady Murray (left) and Zach Parise (center) battle Gabe Gauthier for possession of the puck. The Fighting Sioux hammered DU 6-1 in the opener of a series in frigid North Dakota on January 30, 2004, but the Pioneers rebounded with a 1-1 tie the following night to begin a season-saving nine-game unbeaten streak.

with another loss or two. Soon the only Event they could possibly look forward to was a low seed (and therefore a daunting road trip) in the WCHA playoffs.

Losing was one thing; a few defeats were expected within the unforgiving WCHA slate. What galled several Pioneers was the lack of passion displayed by many of their teammates. Some guys were playing out of position, trying to provide scoring punches when they should have accepted their roles as hard-hitting grinders. Others simply didn't play hard every night. For a team with an abundance of talent but no bona fide superstar, this was a devastating trait. It also was a terrible insult to the legacy of Keith Magnuson, a man who once took boxing lessons to give himself an edge when the gloves came off.

Following the Friday night debacle at North Dakota, the message was as clear as it was simple: Enough is enough. Several temper filled players-only meetings were held. Grievances and criticisms were aired. No quarter was given. Every player's personal pride and ambitions were ignored in the interest of complete honesty. Before the Pioneers could press forward they had to finally work from the same page. If they had to battle each other in order to find that page, so be it.

"Our problem was that we did-

Forward Greg Keith, having a discussion with Colorado College's Aaron Slattengren, was one of many seniors who aired their grievances during a series of team meetings in North Dakota. Keith realized the Pioneers had to come together as a group before they could come together on the ice.

n't all buy into the same program," said Greg Keith, whose no-holds-barred, reckless abandon style of play hadn't caught on with many teammates. "Guys were trying to do their own thing. I guess it was at the end of January that everyone decided that you might have been a goal scorer in junior hockey, but now you're a third-line checker and that's what you're going to do. We all finally bought into it."

Already irritated by their sluggish play, DU was rankled further by an ungracious situation which prevented their taking any practice time on Saturday morning. The Pioneers passed the day by working their tempers out in the weight room and venting further frustrations in more team meetings. Somewhere amid all the raging testosterone the team matured. That night would see the debut of the new Pioneers.

Adam Berkhoel turned in one of his best games of the regular season at North Dakota on January 31, 2004, stopping 30 shots by the Fighting Sioux to help the Pioneers earn a 1-1 draw.

A focused Gwozdecky had little to say to the team. For once he was having difficulty getting a read on his players. Instead of trying to figure it out with a routine pregame speech, Gwozdecky drove his message home with a few simple words scribbled on the chalkboard.

Play Hard.
Play Smart.
Play Together.

For perhaps the first time all season, the Pioneers did all three. Denver's defense limited the Fighting Sioux to seven first-period shots, half as many as they allowed the night before. Though Zach Parise, North Dakota's other Hobey Baker hopeful, put the Sioux on the board midway through the first period of the finale, Berkhoel and his defensemen had finally solved North Dakota's attack. After being thoroughly outshot in the first three games against the Fighting Sioux, the Pioneers claimed a 15-12 shot advantage in the third period. With the offense clicking in the third period for the first time in months, Caldwell evened the score at the 6:20 mark with his ninth goal of the season.

The Pioneers came up empty during a flurry of chances late in the third period and in overtime, and had to settle for a draw. Although the Pioneers remained in the lower half of the WCHA standings, netting a point in the face of such overwhelming adversity helped resurrect their crippled confidence. More importantly, the team discovered a blueprint for success that would carry them to unforeseeable heights. They finally understood that defense was the name of the game.

"At North Dakota, we lost that first game and I got pulled in the first 11 minutes," Berkhoel said. "We sat down after the game and said we needed to start calling guys out. We needed to start focusing on our own thing and quit getting on guys. That Saturday, when we tied them 1-1, that really set the tone. It gave us a chance to know that we can play with the best teams in the country. I think that was a big part of our season. Guys started looking in the mirror and taking it upon themselves. When you made a mistake, you took the blame."

It was fitting that Caldwell scored the game-tying goal against the Fighting Sioux shortly after leading the Pioneers through enough team meetings to start a self-help group. Inspired by his own raging competitive fire, as well as the lessons learned during John Coombe's leadership seminars, Caldwell was beginning to spread his wings as a captain. Few DU captains have combined the grit of a warrior with the laid-back wit of a class clown, as Caldwell did. Chronically aching knees kept Caldwell out of practice for most of the second half of the season, yet he didn't miss a game after sitting out the Alaska Anchorage match on January 24th.

Caldwell no longer could complete his in-season workouts, and his weight began to drop. Never the most burly defender in the first place, his shrinking frame still did not affect his play. In fact, Caldwell's production only got better as his knees got worse. In the months to follow his knack for breaking tense on-ice moments with whimsical quips helped DU handle the increasing pressure they faced as they progressed on the national stage.

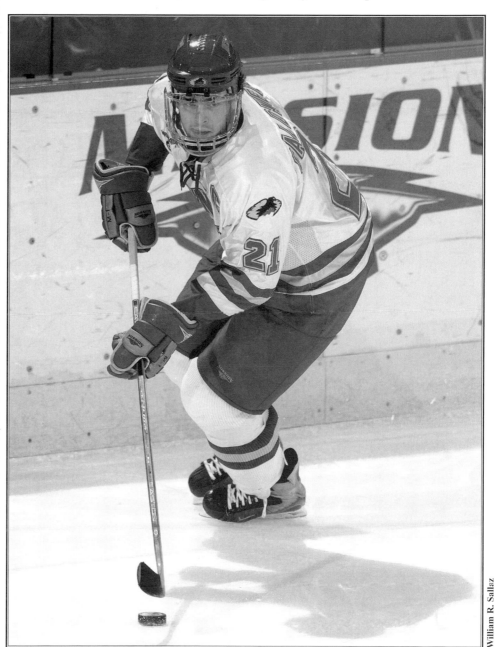

Ryan Caldwell met future DU teammate Max Bull when the pair played at Shattuck-St. Mary's Prep School in Minnesota.

Caldwell's development into the kind of player who could crack jokes while smearing an opposing forward against the glass really was not a surprise. He had been making a point of having fun with hockey since he first donned skates beside the frozen ponds of his rustic hometown of Deloraine, Manitoba.

"I started playing with my dad when I was five," Caldwell said. "I'm from a town of 900 people, so any 13 kids who had a pair of skates were on the team. For me, growing up playing hockey was always fun. It was just the kids from your hometown and it wasn't too serious. I never came from the select background, playing on all the select teams and being the best player all the time. Growing up in a small town, and having the ability to skate whenever I wanted, definitely helped me get better as a player. I wouldn't trade my hockey background for anything."

Caldwell hardly was an immediate superstar. He was cut from several select teams during his early teens before eventually landing on Andy Murray's team at Shattuck-St. Mary's Prep School. Caldwell and future DU teammate Max Bull helped lead that club to the Midget National Championship in 1999, and the following season Caldwell joined the Thunder Bay Flyers of the USHL.

Caldwell arrived in Denver the following year and made an immediate impact. He earned a spot on the WCHA's All-Rookie team after sharing the team lead with 20 assists and posting 23 points, the most by any of the Pioneers' blueliners. But Caldwell also logged a team-leading 76 penalty minutes, a feat he repeated the following year.

Caldwell cut his penalty minutes to 58 during his junior season, and though his presence in the penalty box remained common during his senior year, the captain managed to eliminate many of the silly, ill-timed penalties that marked his first three seasons. In 2003-04 his leadership skills seemed to improve with every shift. His drive, maturity, and education from the John Coombe-led leadership seminars emerged just when DU most needed guidance.

"With him being such an easy-going person, it was easy for some of the younger guys to approach him," junior defenseman Matt Laatsch said. "He made things fun in the locker room, but he still knew when to be serious. He led by example and was a leader on and off the ice. But he also had great support from his senior class. You can't be an effective leader without the guys behind you giving support."

The Pioneers enjoyed a much-needed bye following the North Dakota series, their second bye in four weeks, yet they remained seven points behind the coveted fifth spot in the WCHA standings. They returned to the ice for a home series against Minnesota State, Mankato. Motivated by the chance to make amends for the injury-riddled fiasco against the Mavericks

William R. Sallaz

Jon Foster was one of DU's top offensive threats on the power play, finishing second on the team with seven power play goals. Foster propelled DU to a sweep of Minnesota State in February by scoring two goals in the series opener.

in late December, Caldwell cemented his leadership in what proved to be another monumental series for DU.

Unlike the night of DU's surreal breakdown at Mankato, the Pioneers came into the series with Gwozdecky behind the bench and a full lineup unaffected by injury. Denver dominated the series opener, a 7-1 victory sparked by two goals apiece from juniors Jon Foster and Jeff Drummond. Berkhoel was denied his fifth shutout of the season when the Mavericks scored with 16 seconds remaining, yet the lopsided victory gave the Pioneers 18 goals in three games against Minnesota State; they had every reason to believe they would record their first

Rocky Mountain News

FORWARD THINKING AIDS DU'S VICTORY

Saturday, February 14, 2004
By Pat Rooney
SPECIAL TO THE NEWS

Jon Foster and Jeff Drummond personify the type of up-and-down season the University of Denver hockey team has weathered this year.

At times, the junior forwards have provided the Pioneers with impact plays on offense, lending scoring support to offensive mainstays such as Connor James and Lukas Dora. Other times, the duo has been almost invisible, with each skater suffering through extended goal-scoring droughts this season.

On Friday, Drummond and Foster put together their most prolific games this season. The Pioneers had their best all-around offensive performance since December in a 7-1 win against Minnesota State-Mankato at Magness Arena.

Foster, Drummond and freshman Matt Carle each scored two goals, while goalkeeper Adam Berkhoel made 22 saves and narrowly missed the 10th shutout of his career, when Mankato finally got on the board with 16 seconds remaining.

The win pulled DU even with Colorado College in the Western Collegiate Hockey Association standings, a position the Pioneers can improve on when they face the Mavericks in the series finale tonight (7, Fox Sports Net).

"All the forwards are just trying to throw the puck at the net," Foster said. "It just happened to go in for me and Jeff (on Friday), and the team really fed off of us."

Foster started the scoring in the first period, posting his first goal in seven games after shrugging off Mankato defender Steven Johns to create a one-on-one opportunity against Mavericks goalkeeper Jon Volp.

DU (17-10-4, 7-10-4 WCHA) took the 1-0 lead into the second period, where the Pioneers scored three times to take control. Drummond scored both his goals on rebounds during power-play opportunities, increasing his total to 12.

Foster pushed home a loose puck in between Drummond's tallies to post his first two-goal game since scoring twice in the first game of his freshman season more than two years ago. Foster now has 11 goals this season.

"Those were definitely garbage (goals)," said Drummond, who had not enjoyed a two-goal game since the first game of the year. "When you go to the net and drive into the middle of the lane, you're going to get scoring chances."

Carle scored twice in the third period, with fellow freshman Adrian Veideman adding his fourth goal of the season to complete the scoring for DU. Carle also collected two assists. Veideman also had an assist to earn his first career multiple-point game. DU junior Kevin Ulanski collected a pair of assists.

The Pioneers outshot the Mavericks 41-23 and killed eight of Mankato's nine power-play opportunities.
"We played with a great amount of intensity," DU coach George Gwozdecky said. "Our team really knew what was at stake going into this series."

home sweep of a WCHA series the following night.

And, indeed, DU did just that. But not before surviving another improbable scenario that Gwozdecky believes was one of the turning points of the season.

Though the Mavericks skated to a quick 1-0 lead, Caldwell scored twice in a four-goal barrage that closed the first period. Minnesota State got within 4-2 less than a minute into the second period, but goals by Bull and Gabe Gauthier extended DU's lead to 6-2 going into the third period.

This, however, remained the same Mavericks team that scored four goals in less than eight minutes during their frenetic rally against DU in December. Gwozdecky respectfully compared the Mavericks to cockroaches because of their annoying ability to stay alive in the face of any deficit. In the third period they showed once again that a four-goal margin is hardly enough repellent to keep them buried under the floorboards.

Early in the third period Minnesota State scored three goals within 75 seconds. A goal by Foster stemmed the tide momentarily, but the Mavericks tied the game with two more goals in a span of 81 seconds.

Sophomore defenseman Brett Skinner emerged as a major scoring threat along the blueline, recording 30 points on seven goals and 23 assists.

William R. Sallaz

With less than four minutes remaining the stunned Pioneers found themselves in a 7-7 game. Minnesota State had done this before, and the memories of DU's recent Saturday night third-period letdowns at home remained painfully clear. Yet so did the harsh words the team shared two weeks earlier at North Dakota. On this particular Saturday night at Magness Arena, in this third period, DU would finally turn things around.

"One thing the guys have to be proud of is that instead of packing our tents and folding it in once Mankato tied it up, we responded," Keith said. "We got a big goal, something we really needed. I think at the beginning of the season we might not have been able to do that. Now we were able to fight through the adversity and score a big one."

It was Gauthier who scored the big goal, perhaps the biggest goal of the year when it came to regenerating the Pioneers' confidence. Gauthier's goal, his 11th of the year, came off an assist from Skinner with 1:10 remaining. Caldwell sealed the win and completed his first career hat trick with an empty net goal in the final seconds,

William R. Sallaz

Freshman forward Mike Handza recorded his first career goal during DU's 3-0 win at Michigan Tech on February 21, 2004. Handza was one of only three DU skaters to play in all 44 games.

sparking a celebration that saw several dozen caps rain down on the ice. Caldwell now had 12 goals in 30 games after coming into the season with 11 goals in 114 games. The Pioneers finally completed their first sweep of a WCHA series at home, giving them a modest three-game unbeaten streak. Confidence, as well as physical health, had reached new peaks in Denver's dressing room.

"Our guys were so relieved to get that monkey off our back," Gwozdecky said. "I think that game really had a lot to do with us regaining our confidence, regaining that idea that we could win tight games."

The Pioneers felt the tide shifting after recording their first third-period comeback win of the season. For once, anything seemed possible.

"That was a big part of the turning point of our season," Berkhoel said. "We had struggled against Mankato over the years, and them coming back from that 7-1 deficit in December really knocked us off track for part of the year. When they came back and tied it, we said it wasn't going to happen again. To beat them 9-7 and keep on a run was huge for us."

Backed by momentum for the first time all year, the sixth-place Pioneers set their sights on climbing into the top half of the league standings, a position that would secure home ice in the first round of the WCHA playoffs. Six games remained in the regular season, yet with so much ground to make up each one essentially was a playoff game. If they weren't all must-wins, they were games they couldn't lose; just one more defeat would likely force the Pioneers to begin the WCHA tournament on the road for the second consecutive year.

The stretch run commenced in frustrating fashion, as a trip to last-place Michigan Tech began with a 1-1 tie. Kevin Ulanski put DU on the board early in the first period, but the Pioneers couldn't finish another scoring chance despite a 37-24 shot advantage. Nothing short of two points would suffice in the series finale, and Denver collected them with a 3-0 win. Freshman Mike Handza capped Denver's three-goal second period with his first career goal. Berkhoel made 30 saves to notch his fifth shutout of the year.

DU CHASES AWAY THIRD-PERIOD BLUES

Saturday, February 28, 2004
By Pat Rooney
SPECIAL TO THE NEWS

The University of Denver hockey team has not always been at its best in the third period this season.

Opponents have scored three goals in the final frame against the Pioneers seven times this year. So when Minnesota scored early in the third period during the two teams' series opener Friday, it would have been understandable for DU to wonder if lightning was going to strike yet again.

But DU is enjoying its best stretch of consistent hockey this season, and like many of the shortcomings that have kept the Pioneers from breaking loose, it appears as if the team's third-period woes are a thing of the past. The Pioneers answered Minnesota's late challenge with a pair of game-breaking goals that secured a 6-2 victory at Magness Arena.

The win extended the Pioneers' unbeaten streak to six games and put the squad within two points of fifth-place Minnesota in the Western Collegiate Hockey Association standings. DU can pull into a tie with the Golden Gophers - and claim the tiebreaker against them as well - with a victory tonight in the series finale (7, Comcast Cable channel 5).

"(Friday), our third period was typical of what we've been doing in the third period since that Mankato game," said DU coach George Gwozdecky, referring to a 9-7 victory by DU on Feb. 14 despite surrendering five third-period goals. "We were patient. We knew (Minnesota) would have to press, and we knew we would be able to get some chances if we were smart with the puck and caught them out of position."

DU (20-10-5, 10-10-5 WCHA) scored twice in each period, getting two goals from Connor James, and collecting a goal and two assists from Brett Skinner, the first three-point game of the sophomore defenseman's career. Minnesota took a 1-0 lead on a goal by Jake Fleming before the game was 3 minutes old, but the Pioneers answered with goals by Jeff Drummond and James to take a 2-1 edge at the first intermission.

Luke Fulghum's 10th goal of the season gave DU a 3-1 lead early in the second period and also chased Minnesota goaltender Kellen Briggs, who allowed three goals on six shots. A goal by Gabe Gauthier - his team-leading 14th - gave the Pioneers a 4-1 edge entering the third.

Minnesota, the two-time defending national champions, received a power-play goal from Thomas Vanek early in the third to trim DU's lead to 4-2. But the Pioneers' defense withstood Minnesota's rally. James and Skinner scored 42 seconds apart midway through the period to secure the victory.

Minnesota (20-12-3, 13-11-1 WCHA) outshot the Pioneers 29-28 but could not solve DU goaltender Adam Berkhoel, who recorded 27 saves to run his record to 17-9-4.

"We're playing hard for 60 minutes, and we're getting great goaltending," Skinner said. "We've learned from our mistakes before. (Tonight) is going to be a battle for both teams. We're playing for home-ice advantage, and so are they. We just have to come out with the same intensity and work hard for the full 60."

Though they earned three points, the Pioneers remained in sixth place with four games to go. DU's next challenge was a home series against two-time defending NCAA champ University of Minnesota, which led the Pioneers by four points in the WCHA standings. Denver split its first WCHA series of the year at Minnesota four months earlier, yet by now the Pioneers were morphing into a completely different team. Their troubles at home and in the third period were officially healed. With the voracity of pit bulls Denver unleashed its energy on Minnesota goaltender Kellen Briggs, a native of Colorado Springs who had a miserable homecoming.

In the series opener it took Drummond only 28 seconds to answer an early Minnesota score, and James' ninth goal of the season gave DU a 2-1 edge at the end of the first period. Luke Fulghum scored at the 2:14 mark of the second period, forcing Briggs to the bench with three goals allowed in six shots. James later added his second goal of the game to lead Denver's 6-2 win.

The following night featured a repeat performance. Fulghum and Keith scored early in the first period, sending Briggs back to the sideline with two goals in four shots. Matt Carle produced his second four-point game of the season to lead a 6-3 victory. Its defense now getting better every week, Denver's offense came through with two goals in each of the six periods against the two-time national champs.

"It's coming down to the last few games of the season, and we have to keep playing well if we want to contend for the WCHA tournament and the national title," Fulghum said after recording two goals and an assist in the sweep of the Golden Gophers. "We have no choice but to continue playing hard. "

Senior wing Connor James, shown here earlier against Minnesota-Duluth, broke out of a scoring slump by recording three goals and an assist during DU's sweep of two-time defending national champion Minnesota.

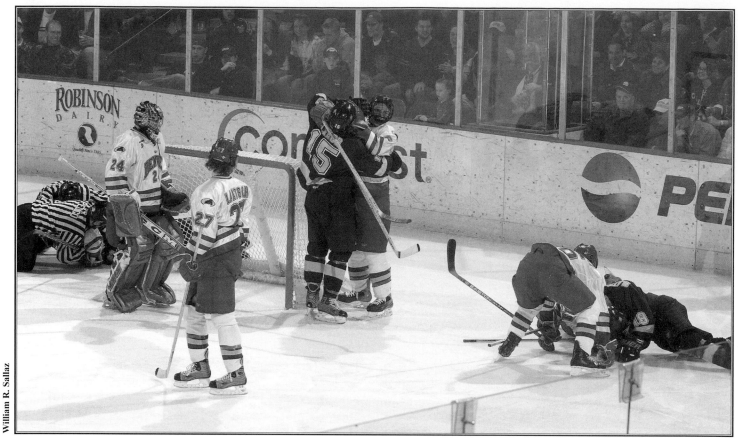

William R. Sallaz

DU and Colorado College first played in 1950, when the Tigers rolled to a 16-0 victory. The rivalry has only become more heated since, and the Gold Pan was introduced in 1993 as a symbol of state bragging rights.

The most impressive sweep of the season increased the Pioneers' unbeaten streak to seven games. The four points pushed DU into a fifth-place tie with Minnesota, but with three wins in four games against the Golden Gophers, the Pioneers owned the tie-breaker. With one regular season series remaining, DU suddenly was in position to capture fourth place, which St. Cloud State held by one point over the Pioneers.

While Minnesota hosted St. Cloud State on the final weekend of the regular season, Denver would attempt to win back the Gold Pan with another home-and-home series against arch rival Colorado College.

Since the 1993-94 season, Denver and Colorado College have competed for the Gold Pan, an authentic mining tool that bestows bragging rights upon the victor of the regular season series. In addition to the series' ramifications on the league playoff picture, the Pioneers also had their eyes set on recapturing the Gold Pan, a prize they had not owned since 1999. Because the Gold Pan has to be won outright from its possessor, one loss would ruin DU's chances for the Pan and also dampen its hopes for home ice in the WCHA tournament.

The series began on a Thursday night at the Colorado Springs World Arena, where the Pioneers continued to show how comfortable they were on the venue's Olympic-sized surface. Gauthier and Fulghum, who attended Coronado High School in Colorado Springs, each scored in the second period to give Denver a 2-1 edge going into the third period. James scored his 12th goal of the season in the final minute, securing a 3-1 victory that extended the Pioneers' unbeaten streak to eight games.

The Pioneers only needed a tie in the regular season finale to regain the Gold Pan, but a win would clinch fourth place in the WCHA. They achieved both goals by completing their late-season surge with another cold-blooded third period performance.

Goals by Keith and J.D. Corbin staked DU to a 2-0 lead, but the Tigers answered with two consecutive goals that tied the game midway through the third. The game crept toward overtime when a Colorado College penalty gave Denver a power play opportunity with just over five minutes remaining. Caldwell again came up with a clutch play, ending a flurry in front of Colorado College's net with his 13th goal of the year. Denver weathered the final 3:27 to complete the sweep in a bitter contest that saw the rivals pummel each other for a combined 87 penalty minutes.

Denver regained possession of the Gold Pan for the first time in five years. DU had won five in a row and owned a nine-game unbeaten streak. The Pioneers averaged 4.3 goals during the streak, and in those nine games Berkhoel compiled a 1.96 goals against average while posting a .933 saves percentage. Carle was the leading point-producer during the nine-game surge, tallying 16 points. The team killed 38 of their opponents' 41 power play chances during the streak.

"In my opinion, the North Dakota game is the benchmark game," assistant coach Steve Miller said, referring to the tie that began the nine-game unbeaten streak. "Everything rolled from there. Beating Minnesota State, Mankato on that Saturday was huge in a game where they stole the momentum from us, but we won it back. When we beat Minnesota and Colorado College back-to-back, I think our team said, 'We can do anything we want to.'"

Denver vaulted all the way to fourth place in the WCHA, setting up a repeat engagement against Colorado College in the first round of the league playoffs. The Pioneers were almost unanimous in their assessment of what keyed their surprisingly dominant turnaround: tight defense and good health.

"I think it was a matter of getting everybody healthy, especially in the defensive corps," Matt Laatsch said. "Once everybody came back, that's when we started pitching shutouts and playing unbelievable defense. A good offense starts with a good defense. And it starts with Adam Berkhoel, the best goaltender in the country."

The Pioneers toasted their sudden success, though they no longer could toast their good health. Connor James had crashed awkwardly into the wall behind the net during the second period of the regular season finale. He was helped from the ice and did not return. Following the game Denver announced that James had suffered a fractured right fibula, the smaller bone of the lower leg.

The Pioneers' second-leading scorer, who had four goals and an assist in the three games prior to his unfortunate crash, would not be available for the WCHA playoffs. James had not missed a single game in his career,

William R. Sallaz

Adam Berkhoel split goaltending duties for two seasons with Wade Dubielewicz, but he was more than ready to assume the entire load in 2003-04, starting each of DU's final 20 games.

Rocky Mountain News

PIONEERS RIDE DEFENSE TO TOP CC; UNBEATEN STREAK REACHES 9 GAMES

Saturday, March 6, 2004
By Pat Rooney
SPECIAL TO THE NEWS

One of the backbones of the University of Denver hockey team's current winning streak has been its resurgent defense. Rarely has that defense been better this season than it was Friday night against state rival Colorado College.

The Pioneers completed a sweep of the Tigers with a 3-2 victory at Magness Arena, extending their winning streak to nine games and capturing the Gold Pan for the first time in four years.

DU's defense throttled the Tigers throughout the first period before turning in a dominant performance on the penalty kill to keep CC at bay. DU captain Ryan Caldwell scored the winning goal with 3 minutes, 27 seconds remaining, jamming home his 13th goal of the season during a five-on-three power play.

The celebration was muted, though, after the game, when the Pioneers learned that second-leading scorer Connor James suffered a season-ending broken right fibula. The victory, combined with Minnesota's win against St. Cloud, secures the fourth seed for DU in the Western Collegiate Hockey Association tournament, which begins next week.

The bad blood between the longtime rivals, which resulted in 26 roughing penalties Friday, will continue when seventh-place CC returns to Magness on Friday to begin a best-of-three first-round series against the Pioneers.

"We're not taking shifts off like we were earlier in the year," said DU goaltender Adam Berkhoel, who recorded his 20th win of the season. "It was an unbelievable effort by our D-corps, especially our penalty kill. We didn't give them much at all, especially on their five-on-threes."

DU (23-10-5, 13-10-5 WCHA) held the Tigers to only one shot in the first 18 minutes, while outshooting CC 21-3 in the first period. The Pioneers killed all five of CC's power-play opportunities, which included a combined stretch during the first two periods of 3:15 in which the Tigers enjoyed a five-on-three advantage.

DU has killed 38 of its opponents' 41 power-play chances during its winning streak. Colorado College (18-15-3, 11-15-2 WCHA) has wallowed at the other extreme, going scoreless in its past 22 power-play opportunities.

"I think defense and penalty killing all come down to goaltending, and Adam has been playing out of his mind for a month now," Caldwell said. "He makes us look good."

Greg Keith put DU on the board, scoring his ninth goal of the season during a five-on-three power play early in the first period. The Pioneers extended their lead to 2-0, when speedy freshman J.D. Corbin raced down the left wing to score his third goal of the year.

CC captain Colin Stuart kept the Tigers in the game, cutting the deficit to 2-1 with a goal midway through the second period, before tying the score with his ninth goal of the year with 9:47 remaining in the third. Although Caldwell's late goal allowed DU's seven seniors to enjoy possession of the Gold Pan for the first time in their careers, the achievement was dulled somewhat by James' injury.

"It was the strangest game in I don't know how long for me," DU coach George Gwozdecky said. "The last 30 minutes was the Adam Berkhoel show. He was outstanding."

but the only way that career would continue was if Denver could somehow reach the Frozen Four. Despite the team's late turnaround, most people believed James had skated in his last game for Denver.

"Connor brought a lot to the table. He brought a lot of offensive skill through his passing, goal scoring, and his speed," Fulghum said. "We're just going to have to make do without and battle through it. We're going to miss him greatly because he is one of our best players."

Gwozdecky was confident that his team had navigated enough hurdles that the loss of James would not be as disastrous as it might have been in December.

"As a team, we have met countless challenges throughout the season. We've overcome those challenges, and this is another one that we are going to meet head-on and overcome."

The state rivals regrouped for their first opening-round showdown since 1998 with vastly different mindsets. Barring an unlikely array of nation-wide upsets, Denver's dominant nine-game unbeaten streak had all but assured it of an NCAA tournament berth. Colorado College, on the other hand, was fighting for its postseason life. The Tigers were a legitimate bubble team that needed

Monty Rand Photography

Sophomore Ted O'Leary, a native Coloradoan, replaced injured senior Connor James in the WCHA playoffs and responded with his first career goal in the first game against Colorado College.

every win they could muster. The Pioneers were drained from the playoff atmosphere they had competed in for the past two months, and the absence of James meant they would play without one of their most skilled attackers when the series opened at Magness Arena on March 12.

The first career goal by Arvada native Ted O'Leary, who filled James' spot in the lineup, plus a goal by Gauthier, gave Denver a 2-1 lead going into the third period. Then, as though stricken by a fast-acting virus, Denver suffered what psychologists call a relapse, allowing three goals in a span of 4:26 during the third period to enable Colorado College to escape with a 4-3 victory.

The Pioneers expected to rebound the following night. But they were fatigued, and the hungry Tigers didn't wait until the third period to start goal-hunting around Berkhoel's crease, opening Game 2 with three consecutive goals. Gwozdecky replaced Berkhoel with Glenn Fisher in the final two minutes of the frame, but the move couldn't prevent a lopsided 6-1 Colorado College victory that sent the Tigers to the WCHA Final Five.

The abrupt exit stunned the Pioneers' fans, who thought they had seen the last of this kind of third-period shelling. Apparently ignorant of the nine-game unbeaten streak that had already saved the season, one disgruntled student season-ticket holder hurled a T-shirt at the DU bench that read: "FIRE GWOZDECKY." Berkhoel was despondent over his performance, which would become a source of inspiration in the ensuing weeks.

"When the team is playing bad, I'm supposed to be there to bail them out. And I did not bail them out one bit," Berkhoel said. "I take the blame. We just pretty much gave them that game. I don't know what else to say."

The coaching staff ordered the Pioneers to be ready for practice on Monday. While their dreams for a WCHA championship were over, a greater prize was still out there for the taking. Although they would have to wonder about where they would go, the Pioneers were still ranked sixth in the PairWise Rankings, which replicates the method used to select the NCAA tournament field. A bid was all but

Monty Rand Photography

Greg Keith wasn't worried about the Pioneers' failure to advance out of the first round of the WCHA playoffs. He sensed the week off would pay huge dividends.

assured. To a man the Pioneers firmly believed their poor performance in the WCHA playoffs was the result of physical and mental fatigue. Ironically, the Pioneers needed rest more than the bright lights of the WCHA Final Five.

Greg Keith certainly was convinced of that. Roughly an hour after getting bounced from the conference tournament, Keith was leaving Magness Arena while trying to call his parents to inform them of the bad news. When asked about what had just transpired on the ice, Keith simply shrugged and mumbled, "Ah, we'll be okay."

Keith trudged off quietly into the darkened campus, unaware that more prophetic words had never been so casually spoken.

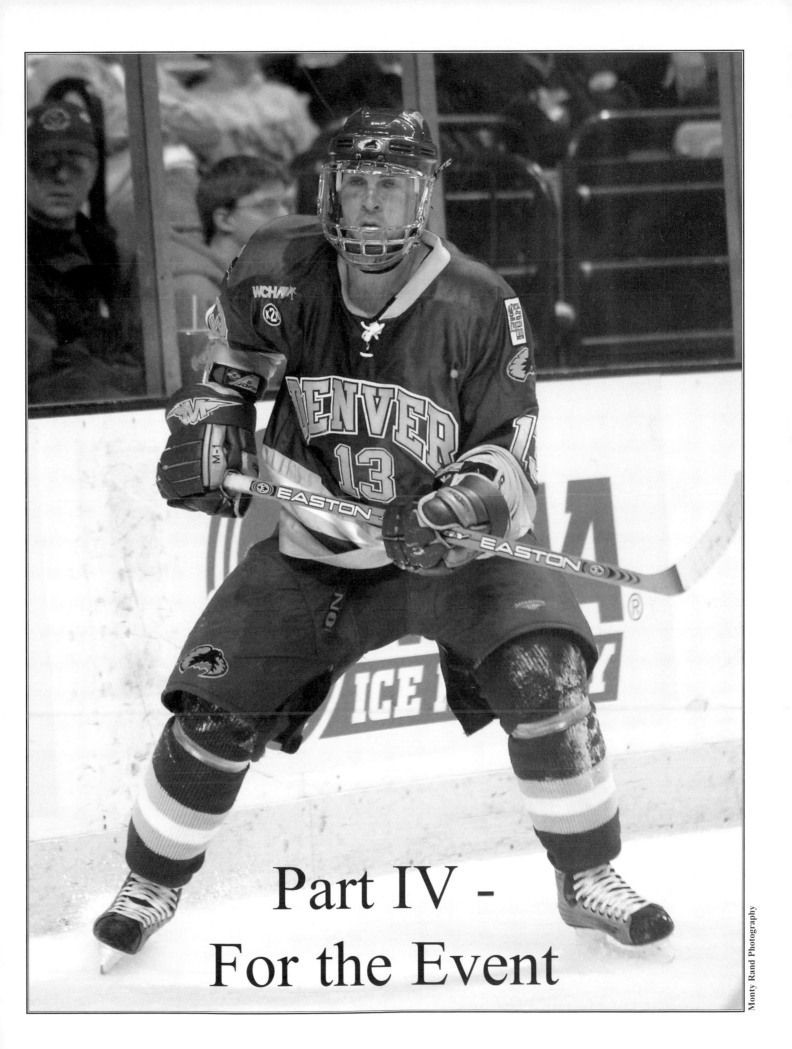

Part IV -
For the Event

Rocky Mountain News

WARM FRIENDSHIPS TO TURN ICY FRIDAY; PALS WILL BE RIVALS AS DU, MIAMI FACE OFF

Thursday, March 25, 2004
By Pat Rooney
SPECIAL TO THE NEWS

University of Denver hockey coach George Gwozdecky and Miami of Ohio coach Rico Blasi share a relationship that goes back about 15 years. That's when Gwozdecky, then Miami's coach, recruited Blasi to play for him.

But when their teams square off Friday night in the NCAA West Regional at Colorado Springs, the coaches will not be the only ones renewing an old friendship.

DU's Ryan Caldwell, a senior defenseman and team captain, played junior hockey with the Thunder Bay Flyers of the U.S. Hockey League. One of his best friends on that team was Mike Kompon, a native of Thunder Bay, Ontario.

Kompon, a senior forward for Miami, and Caldwell likely will have a far more physical reunion than their coaches when the Pioneers begin play in the tournament against the RedHawks at 9 p.m. Friday at the World Arena (Comcast Cable, Channel 5). The winner will play either top-seeded North Dakota or Holy Cross on Saturday for an opportunity to advance to the Frozen Four.

"(Kompon) was one of the other guys that was a rookie on the team, so we hung out quite a bit," said Caldwell, who still shares e-mails with the RedHawk player. "He's a good guy. He's been tearing it up his whole career with (Miami)."

Caldwell certainly won't be as friendly Friday night. Kompon is one of four RedHawks players with at least 35 points, more than all but one of DU's active players. Kompon is tied for second for Miami with 42 points, and his 31 assists are tied for the team lead.

The Pioneers' primary challenge will be slowing Kompon, Greg Hogeboom, Hobey Baker Award finalist Derek Edwardson and Matt Christie, a freshman who has scored a team-most 21 goals. Caldwell believes he and his fellow blue-liners can build on the experience they collected this season in the rugged Western Collegiate Hockey Association.

"When I get him in the corner, I'm going to let him know we're not on the same team anymore," Caldwell said. "I think we can really draw on our experiences playing against North Dakota and Minnesota this year. "We've got a lot of teams that are loaded up front in the WCHA. From a defensive standpoint, you got to be aware of where those guys are on the ice and maybe take chances when they're not on the ice."

For the Pioneers, taking chances probably will involve using their speed to outskate Miami on the expansive Olympic-sized rink at the World Arena. DU beat Colorado College twice this year in the building and played well throughout the season on bigger ice surfaces.

"Their team is a lot better than their coach's golf game is," Gwozdecky said, jokingly. "In fact, their team is really, really good. Christie is a freshman with 21 goals . . . he's good. They are so close to having a lot more good things happen to them this year, and we respect the heck out of that team and what they have been able to accomplish."

Denver vs. Miami (Ohio)
West Regional First Round
Colorado Springs World Arena
March 26, 2004

While the University of Denver's rivals in the Western Collegiate Hockey Association beat each other up at the Final Five in Minnesota, the Pioneers rested and prepared for the NCAA tournament.

The workouts were spirited despite the team's two losses against Colorado College. No one knew how well the team would fare, but everyone agreed the two-week rest would allow the Pioneers to be at their physical peak for college hockey's Big Dance.

"I will go to my grave saying that week off was huge for us," assistant coach Steve Miller said. "If we would have had to play games that weekend, maybe even three games...I just don't know what would have happened."

The break allowed the Pioneers to treat their ailing bodies as they awaited their next challenge. Connor James was one week closer to making a comeback from his broken leg. Ryan Caldwell kicked up his feet, iced his aching knees,

The week off between their WCHA playoff loss and the start of the NCAA tournament was a relief for many DU players. Max Bull (above) used the off-week to recover from a rib injury.

and steeled himself for one more gritty push. And Max Bull, who suffered a painful rib injury against Colorado College that would have kept him out of the lineup for the WCHA finals, slowly regained his strength.

While the humiliating losses to Colorado College left the team pondering its immediate future, a berth in the NCAA tournament essentially was secured with the nine-game unbeaten streak the Pioneers put together at the end of the regular season. DU remained in the top 10 in the PairWise Rankings. The only question still lingering was whether Denver would get to play in the West Regional at Colorado Springs. There was a chance the losses to Colorado College would force the Pioneers to head east.

The hope was that poetic justice would prevail, given the recent history of Colorado teams in the NCAA tournament.

In 2002, DU was one of the favorites to win the national championship and entered the tournament as the top seed in the West Region. The team's so-called reward for becoming the first team in 11 years to win both the WCHA regular season and the league playoffs was an NCAA tournament date with the University of Michigan in Ann Arbor. Their loss in that game still grated on Denver's older players. Colorado College experienced an identical fate in 2003, losing by the same 5-3 count to the Wolverines in the Midwest Regional final at Michigan. With the NCAA tournament returning to Colorado, the Pioneers and their fans were almost demanding a chance to play near home.

Those questions were answered on March 21, when the team, as well as a modest crowd of fans and parents, gathered at the Lazy Dog Bar and Grill near campus to watch the tournament selection show. DU received the second seed in the West Region, behind WCHA regular season champ North Dakota, and the seventh seed overall. Instead of traveling to a hostile, rambunctious rink across the country, the Pioneers would continue The Journey by making the short drive down I-25 to the Colorado Springs World Arena, where they had gone 3-0 during the regular season.

"Where we ended up really didn't matter to us, but being close to home definitely can be an advantage," Caldwell said. "We found that out two years ago when Michigan beat us."

Denver drew Miami (Ohio) for its first round match, a team the Pioneers almost played at the Lefty McFadden Tournament in Ohio at the beginning of the year. The RedHawks were upset by St. Lawrence in the first round of that early-season showcase, preventing a possible preview of the NCAA tournament, yet Denver's coaching staff was hardly unfamiliar with Miami's style and personnel.

Miami coach Rico Blasi is the one person in the college hockey ranks who can claim to be Gwozdecky's star pupil.

The Pioneers faced a familiar opponent in the first round of the NCAA tournament in Miami (Ohio). Kevin Ulanski scored the game-winning goal and added an assist in a 6-0 win against the RedHawks in the Wells Fargo Denver Cup last season.

A native of Weston, Ontario, Blasi was recruited by Gwozdecky when he coached Miami from 1989 to 1994. Blasi was one of Gwozdecky's top players when Miami won its first Central Collegiate Hockey Association crown during the 1992-93 season. Gwozdecky forged an immediate bond with Blasi and his family when he and assistant coach Mike Norton visited the Blasis on a recruiting trip.

"I remember very vividly being in his living room and having dinner with his parents," Gwozdecky said. "Myself and my assistant coach, Mike Norton, were in their home, and we sat down for dinner. Rico's parents are first-generation Italians…when you sit down for a meal, it's a feast. There is course after course after course. You start off with lasagna and pizza, and those are hors d'oeuvres. Grandpa Blasi, he makes his own homemade wine. I'm talking and doing the whole recruiting spiel, and Grandpa Blasi continues to pour wine into Mike's glass. Every time he takes a drink, Grandpa Blasi keeps pouring wine into Mike's glass. An hour into the meal - I'd say at that point we were about halfway done with the meal - Mike is cracking jokes and having a great time. He was close to being four sheets to the wind. So that was a very memorable visit."

Blasi followed Gwozdecky to Denver in 1995, serving one season as a volunteer assistant coach before getting promoted to assistant coach. Gwozdecky, Miller, and Blasi helped build the 1998-99 DU team that fell short of the Frozen Four after losing to - who else? - Michigan in the first game of the NCAA tournament.

University of Miami (Ohio) Athletics

Miami head coach Rico Blasi (back, second from right) played for DU coach George Gwozdecky at the Oxford, Ohio, school and was an assistant under Gwozdecky at Denver. The good friends reunited as adversaries in the NCAA tournament.

Following that season, Blasi was named the head coach at Miami at the tender age of 27. Any controversy surrounding Blasi's hiring was quickly put to rest. The RedHawks won only 13 games during Blasi's first season, but he guided the RedHawks to the best single-season turnaround in the program's history the following year, finishing second in the CCHA with a league mark of 17-10-1.

In 2003-04, Miami went 23-13-4 to earn the team's first NCAA bid since 1997. Blasi would have to make his tournament debut against his mentor, whose team dismantled Blasi's RedHawks 6-0 in their only other head-to-head meeting the previous year.

"Obviously, there is excitement having your team in the tournament, but then there are reservations because you have to play George and Seth and Steve," Blasi said. "Our staffs have spent so much time together. At the same time, you knew someone would lose and have to feel bad afterward."

The familiarity between the coaching staff led to some lighthearted trash-talking leading up to the game.

"If it was staff versus staff on the golf course, we would have a definite advantage. No question about it," Gwozdecky declared. "And we have proven that over the past three years. Their team is a lot better than their coaches' golfing."

Miami entered the West Regional boasting four players who owned at least 35 points. With James side-lined, Gabe Gauthier was the only skater in DU's line-up who could match that production. But Denver was looking forward to the friendlier atmosphere of the Colorado Springs World Arena, and the speedy Pioneers were stoked to play on their in-state rival's Olympic-sized ice sheet. Denver's three victories at the World Arena during the regular season helped build their 8-2-2 mark on the bigger surfaces.

Junior Matt Laatsch was able to overcome an injury-riddled sophomore year to become a reliable part of the defensive rotation. Laatsch gave the Pioneers a 2-0 lead against Miami (Ohio) in the NCAA tournament with a devastating wrist shot.

William R. Sallaz

"When you've had luck somewhere you want to keep going back," Matt Laatsch said. "It just plays to our game. We're a good skating team, a fast team, with quick forwards up front. It has just worked out well for us, that ice."

That trend continued against the RedHawks in the type of adrenaline-pumping game that would become the norm for Denver in the NCAA tournament.

Captain Caldwell put the Pioneers on the board at the 7:01 mark of the first period on a short-handed chance begun by Adrian Veideman and Gauthier. The puck eventually landed on the stick of Caldwell, who wheeled out from behind the net to score his 14th goal of the season off an assist from Lukas Dora.

It was the Pioneers' 10th and final short-handed goal of the season, which tied for the third-most in the nation.

Laatsch put the Pioneers ahead 2-0 early in the second period with a nasty wrist shot off a faceoff won by Veideman. The two goals were all Adam Berkhoel would need. Almost.

Berkhoel, making his first career start in the NCAA tournament, began his sparkling postseason run by turning away 21 RedHawks shots. Miami got to within one when a streaking Marty Guerin beat Berkhoel on a breakaway chance midway through the second period, but DU's defense would limit Miami's opportunities the rest of the way.

The Pioneers again used their special teams to their advantage early in the third period. Sophomore defenseman Brett Skinner put DU ahead 3-1 at the 6:35 mark with a power-play goal off assists from Matt Carle and Gauthier, giving three different defensemen goals in the team's tournament opener. A fluke play during a Miami

Monty Rand Photography

Sophomore Brett Skinner scored the game-winning goal against Miami (Ohio) in the first game of the West Regional. Defensemen accounted for all of the Pioneers' goals in DU's 3-2 victory.

power play allowed the RedHawks to get within a goal with 2:23 remaining, as a clearing pass by Laatsch deflected off Lukas Dora's thigh and whistled past a surprised Berkhoel.

Unfortunately for the RedHawks that stroke of luck was the best scoring chance they could produce against Berkhoel after Guerin's breakaway. The senior goalie was aided by a defensive effort that limited the RedHawks to only 23 shots.

Berkhoel's play left Blasi believing anything was possible for his mentor's team.

"We felt, and I'm sure Denver did too, that if we could get out of the Colorado Springs regional, we had a shot at doing some good things," Blasi said. "You could just tell they were getting more and more confident. Berkhoel was playing well, and Caldwell was just a bear against us."

"Adam Berkhoel continues to give us the goaltending we expect," Gwozdecky said after defeating his prize pupil. "Some would say that many of those saves were unbelievable, but I would say it was just Adam Berkhoel. I've said all along that this is a goaltender's tournament, and we have the best goaltender in the country."

No doubt Gwozdecky's boast drew some scoffs, particularly from fans of Brown's Yann Danis and Maine's Jimmy Howard. Soon, however, Berkhoel would show the nation that his coach was preaching the truth.

Monty Rand Photography

Adam Berkhoel showed no signs of nerves in his NCAA tournament debut, stopping 21 shots and helping to kill four Miami (Ohio) power-play chances to lead DU's 3-2 win.

Rocky Mountain News

DU GAINS WEST FINAL

Saturday, March 27, 2004
By Pat Rooney
SPECIAL TO THE NEWS

COLORADO SPRINGS - Adam Berkhoel promised his teammates he would play more like himself and less like the player who had to be pulled from his previous start.

The University of Denver senior goaltender delivered on that promise Friday night at the Colorado Springs World Arena.

Making his first start in the NCAA tournament, Berkhoel made 21 saves to lead DU to a 3-2 win against Miami (Ohio) University.

The victory also gave Pioneers coach George Gwozdecky, once the coach at Miami, bragging rights over his star pupil-RedHawks coach Rico Blasi, who played for Gwozdecky at the Oxford, Ohio, school and later served as an assistant at DU.

The Pioneers will play top-seeded North Dakota in the regional final tonight at the World Arena (7, Comcast Cable channel 68). The Pioneers have not defeated the Fighting Sioux in their past six meetings, although DU earned a 1-1 draw Jan. 31 at Grand Forks, N.D.

A win against the Fighting Sioux would give the Pioneers their first berth in the NCAA Frozen Four since 1986.

Berkhoel surrendered three first-period goals in DU's previous game, a 6-1 loss against Colorado College on March 13 that eliminated the Pioneers from the Western Collegiate Hockey Association playoffs.

But the Woodbury, Minn. product was sharp Friday, leading a defensive effort that killed six of Miami's seven power-play opportunities and limited the RedHawks to 23 shots.

Berkhoel was spectacular at times, making a stellar kick save against Miami's Taylor Hustead late in the first period and snatching a shot out of the air at the second-period buzzer after losing his stick in front of the crease.

The Pioneers got on the board at the 7-minute, 1-second mark of the first period after taking advantage of the RedHawks' overzealous power-play unit. Gabe Gauthier and freshman Adrian Veideman led a shorthanded charge, with the puck eventually finding the stick of senior defenseman Ryan Caldwell.

Caldwell fired a shot under the crossbar that beat Miami goaltender Brandon Crawford-West for his 14th goal of the year. The tally also was DU's 10th shorthanded goal of the season, moving the Pioneers into a tie with Mercyhurst with the third-most in the nation.

DU (24-12-5) took its 1-0 edge into the second period and quickly added to its lead. Veideman won a faceoff at the left circle in the RedHawks' zone, with junior defenseman Matt Laatsch controlling the puck beyond the arc. From there Laatsch fired a line drive past a screened Crawford-West, extending DU's lead to 2-0.

But Miami needed less than 5 minutes to get back within a goal. Crawford-West stopped DU freshman Matt Carle on a one-on-one chance, with the rebound resulting in a RedHawks rush the other way. Miami's Brian Sipotz fed the puck ahead to a streaking Marty Guerin, who raced past the Pioneers' defense. Guerin beat Berkhoel for his 14th goal of the year, keeping the RedHawks within a goal going into the final period.

The Pioneers put away the game in the third period after a pair of Miami penalties gave DU a five-on-three advantage. Brett Skinner blasted home his seventh goal of the year off assists by Carle and Gabe Gauthier. It was the eighth game in a row in which Carle has recorded an assist.

The RedHawks got within 3-2 with 2:23 remaining when Miami's Matt Davis was credited for a goal when a deflected clearing pass by DU ricocheted into the net, but DU's defense held the rest of the way.

"We saw a little something on tape about the way they play, but it's also something we are trying to stress," assistant coach Seth Appert said. "The key was our forecheck. Our forwards and our defense did a really good job of not backing off the blueline and letting teams skate in the zone and set up on the power play. We were forcing teams to dump the puck. And once we forced teams to dump, we did a great job surrounding the puck. We thought those were the two keys to the penalty kill."

Berkhoel and North Dakota goalie Jordan Parise matched save-for-save throughout a third period that saw the Fighting Sioux once again outshoot the Pioneers, this time by a dominant margin of 10-4. But total shots are meaningless compared to the number that reach the net, and among Denver's four third-period shots was a laser beam by Bull that doomed the team he grew up cheering for.

With under three minutes remaining, junior Luke Fulghum, a native of Colorado Springs who was playing in front of his hometown crowd, worked the puck into the North Dakota zone before leaving it for Lukas Dora. Fulghum crashed the net while Dora used his keen ice presence to locate Bull alone near the top of the left circle. Bull wound up and fired a one-timer, hockey lingo for shooting directly off of a teammates' pass, that left scorch marks across the ice.

"No one really saw me over there. I started screaming and Dora sent it out to me," Bull said. "I didn't have much time to react. We had been practicing that shot from that exact spot. I just ripped it toward the upper right side. I put all 190 pounds of me into the shot and fell to my knees after it."

Bull still likes to call it his goal even though it officially was credited to Fulghum, who re-directed the sizzling puck on its way to the net. The play survived a video review by the officials, and having Fulghum record the goal all but ensured a Denver victory. Once the Pioneers weathered the final 2:29, they improved to 17-0-2 when Fulghum recorded a point.

"My brother was watching with some of his North Dakota friends back in Minnesota," Bull said. "I know when that goal went in my brother got up and started screaming in the middle of the bar. He called right away to congratu-

Junior Luke Fulghum, who grew up in Colorado Springs, wowed his hometown crowd and stunned UND goalie Jordan Parise by tipping in a shot by Max Bull to record DU's only goal in its 1-0 victory in the regional final.

Tom Kimmell

late me. I have to say it probably took another two or three weeks for other friends that are North Dakota fans to say congratulations. It couldn't have been any better for me. I'll see a lot of those guys in the summer, and I'm glad I'll get to see them as a winner."

The play that spawned the winning goal made assistant coaches Seth Appert and Steve Miller beam with pride. Throughout the season many of the Pioneers, Bull included, were guilty of squeezing the stick too tightly on shot opportunities. Bull's monumental one-timer was the culmination of months of drills conducted by Appert and Miller in hopes of improving that exact skill.

"We would do almost that exact play maybe twice a week the whole last half of the season," Appert said. "We weren't necessarily looking for that particular play, but that skill. It is really hard to hit a one-timer cleanly and get a lot on it. We felt our guys weren't shooting well on one-timers and that was something we were really working on."

The 1-0 win gave Berkhoel his sixth shutout of the season and the 11th of his career. Denver advanced to the Frozen Four for the first time since 1986, earning a date with another WCHA rival, Minnesota-Duluth, in the national semifinals.

As Gwozdecky fielded questions following the biggest win of his 10-year tenure at Denver, he made a prediction about the team he would lead into Boston two weeks later by hinting, "We might have a secret weapon by that time."

Somewhere in the corner of the Pioneers' locker room, despite the boot covering his broken leg, a knowing gleam flickered in Connor James' eyes.

Charlie Lengal III

Denver's 1-0 victory in the West Regional final gave the Pioneers their first berth in the Frozen Four since 1986. Adam Berkhoel stopped 54 of 56 shots in the regional to earn the tournament's Most Outstanding Player award.

DU HEADS TO FROZEN FOUR

Saturday, March 27, 2004
By Pat Rooney
SPECIAL TO THE NEWS

COLORADO SPRINGS -It was the biggest goal in years for the University of Denver hockey team. Yet the Pioneers' jubilant victory celebration was just about over in the locker room by the time a consensus was found about which player scored it.

The Pioneers advanced to the Frozen Four for the first time since 1986 with a thrilling 1-0 victory against top-seeded North Dakota in the West Regional final on Saturday. DU used another superb effort by goaltender Adam Berkhoel and a strange late third-period goal to earn the victory.

The Pioneers (25-12-5) will play Sunday's winner between Minnesota and Minnesota-Duluth in the national semifinals on April 8 in Boston. Both teams, like North Dakota, are DU's rivals in the Western Collegiate Hockey Association.

The winning goal eventually was awarded to Colorado Springs native Luke Fulghum, who tipped a laser beam of a shot by senior Max Bull with 2 minutes, 29 seconds remaining in the third period. It was the Pioneers' first win in seven games against the Fighting Sioux.

"The (goals) haven't been coming as easy as they have in the past," said Bull, who earned his 11th assist of the season on the winning play. "I kind of saw the play developing. Lukas (Dora) and Fulghum and me were going into the zone. I just tried to find an open area. Lukas sent it over and I just ripped it as hard as I could."

The only reason the Pioneers were in position to create a game-winning shot was the performance of Berkhoel. The senior netminder earned the regional's MVP award after recording his sixth shutout of the season and the 11th of his career. In two regional games, Berkhoel stopped 54 of 56 shots while improving his season's record to 22-11-4.

"We knew they were going to come out hard and put a lot of (pucks) on us," Berkhoel said. "They are one of the top scoring teams in the country and they put a lot of pucks on the net. Our defense and forwards battled all night and let me see everything. They blocked shots and came back in the zone and tied up guys. It wasn't just me; it was the whole team."

The teams traded scoring chances throughout the contest, though Berkhoel's play allowed DU to overcome North Dakota's 33-17 shot advantage. Each team failed on three power play opportunities, but with neither team taking a penalty in the final frame, the crowd of 6,047 knew the first goal likely would prove to be the game-winner.

The Pioneers got that chance when Fulghum worked the puck into North Dakota's zone and dropped a pass to Dora. The senior from the Czech Republic slid the puck to an open Bull at the left circle. Bull fired a shot that ticked off of Fulghum just enough to fool North Dakota goaltender Jordan Parise.

DU then weathered a final charge by the Fighting Sioux, who pulled Parise with 1: 06 remaining but still could not solve Berkhoel.

"We're not thinking at that point of increasing the lead," DU coach George Gwozdecky said. "We're just going to stay in position properly, because we know they are going to throw everything at us. We had to be in proper defensive position in all areas of the ice."

Denver vs. Minnesota-Duluth
Frozen Four Semifinal
FleetCenter, Boston
April 8, 2004

It was the most important business trip for the Pioneers' program in 18 years, and yet Denver arrived in Boston behaving more like well-to-do tourists than men on a mission.

The Pioneers reveled in their visit to historic Fenway Park and caroused like sailors on shore leave during the police escorts that whisked the team bus through the bustling city traffic. They laughed as often as possible and cranked up the stereo in the dressing room while the other three teams at the Frozen Four - Minnesota-Duluth, Maine, and hometown favorite Boston College - battled nerves.

That's not to say the Pioneers weren't focused on claiming the championship trophy. They simply were following the directives of head coach George Gwozdecky, who ordered his club to savor every moment of the Frozen Four atmosphere. He spoke from experience, having won a national title as a player at Wisconsin in 1977 and adding another as an assistant coach at Michigan State in 1986.

"This is something they worked

Ryan Caldwell's leadership skills culminated in Boston, where the relaxed yet focused Pioneers were able to have fun at the Frozen Four but still keep on the path toward the national championship.

very hard for," Gwozdecky said. "I've seen coaches who have gone the wrong away, where players are not allowed to talk to the media. They tried to stay focused on the task at hand, and even those teams that won it haven't enjoyed the experience as much as they needed to.

"Who knows when anybody with this program will have another opportunity to play in something like this. We want them to enjoy it. When we're not practicing, when we're not meeting, when we're not playing, we want them to be able to enjoy it and smell the roses. We're on the national stage, and this is an experience they will never forget. I want them to be able to enjoy it and not have any regrets. Not only in the games, but in everything else that surrounds us. We want them to have fun and express themselves."

It helped that Gwozdecky truly believed in what he was preaching. Following the regional championship, Gwozdecky spoke with several members of DU's 1986 team, the last Pioneers club to reach the Frozen Four. A few expressed regrets that they had not enjoyed the opportunity as much as they should have; regrets were the last thing Gwozdecky wanted his players to take back to Denver.

Minnesota-Duluth's Junior Lessard, winner of the Hobey Baker Award, put the Pioneers in an early hole with a goal less than two minutes into the national semifinal game.

Predictably, the Pioneers gladly heeded their coach's order. All season they had played their best whenever they took themselves the least seriously. Led by the effervescent Captain Caldwell, the Pioneers focused on enjoying the Boston experience. Several members of the national media unfamiliar with Denver's team commented that the Pioneers' dressing room seemed like a frat party compared to the wakes transpiring in the dressing rooms down the hall.

"I'm so glad that coach said that because that's the kind of guy I am," said Caldwell. "I like to have fun with hockey and joke around in the locker room. The other teams in the tournament, they went in with so many expectations on them and so much pressure. We were the underdogs and we didn't have any of that. We went out there with the attitude that anything can happen and that we might as well have fun until game time. I think that attitude really benefited us. If we had been like the other teams I'm sure the Frozen Four experience, even if we did win, wouldn't have been as fun."

While the Pioneers were completely undaunted by the bright stage, they had reason to fear Minnesota-Duluth in the national semifinals. The Bulldogs featured a high-flying offense that could rival North Dakota. Leading Duluth was forward Junior Lessard, whom Gwozdecky declared was deserving of the Hobey Baker Award about a week before the senior from St. Joseph deBeauce, Quebec, actually collected the trophy.

Lessard, who would sign a free agent contract with the NHL's Dallas Stars days after the Frozen Four, entered the semifinals with 30 goals and 61 points, the best marks in the nation. Linemate Evan Schwabe led the nation with 36 assists and combined with Lessard to produce a goal and an assist apiece during Duluth's two wins at Magness Arena three months earlier. Goalie Isaac Reichmuth was rolling on his own Berkhoel-like streak after stopping 45 of 46 shots in Duluth's two wins at the Midwest Regional.

The game opened with the Pioneers on the defensive; not because of nerves, but because five penalties kept the Bulldogs on the power play for much of the first 12 minutes. Lessard capitalized on a Kevin Ulanski penalty to put Duluth on the board 69 seconds into the game. The Bulldogs made it 2-0 about three and a half minutes later on a goal by Tyler Brosz. After playing so brilliantly in the West Regional, Berkhoel had allowed two goals in the first four shots he faced at the Frozen Four.

Just months earlier the Pioneers probably would have been bracing for a loss somewhere in the 6-1 range. Now they shrugged off Duluth's early foray as if it was a mild annoyance.

"We weren't nervous one bit," claimed Berkhoel. "But we might have gotten a little jittery. Then we sat back and said we're only down 2-0. It wasn't like we were out of the game. We played that laid-back attitude, and once the second period came around the momentum shifted our way."

Denver captured the momentum for good in the second period, posting 12 shots after managing just five in the first. More importantly, the Pioneers' blueliners began to shackle the Bulldogs' potent top line. Denver cut the deficit to 2-1 when Lukas Dora, working behind Duluth's net, fed a charging Luke Fulghum for the junior's 14th goal of the season.

Denver's resurgence almost was squashed when Lessard scored another power play goal on a 2-on-1 charge with Schwabe, giving the Bulldogs a 3-1 edge with 4:25 remaining in the second period. But moments later Berkhoel made a brilliant save against Lessard on a 1-on-1 chance, keeping the Pioneers in the game. That clutch play, combined with the good fortune that always prevailed when

Junior Luke Fulghum gets pumped after scoring DU's first goal of the Frozen Four, converting a pass from Lukas Dora to pull the Pioneers within a goal of the Bulldogs.

Fulghum notched a point, left the Pioneers feeling as if they were in control when they went back to the locker room, despite the two-goal deficit.

Fulghum, who was hoping the Pioneers would improve to 18-0-2 during games in which he scored a point, remembers the typically light-hearted speech the seniors led during the second intermission.

"Max Bull, between the second and third period, said 'You know, guys, we're fine because Fulghum got his point.' At that point, it got us going and made us believe. Stats sometimes don't lie, and that was one of the things that helped us."

Denver charged back to the ice and put together its best third period of the season. Much of the effort was due to the abrupt return to form by Connor James.

DU GLEE PARTY: PIONEERS REACH FIRST FINAL SINCE 1973 WITH THIRD-PERIOD RALLY

Friday, April 9, 2004
By Pat Rooney
SPECIAL TO THE NEWS

BOSTON - Absolutely nothing was going well, and the University of Denver hockey team was on the verge of being routed in college hockey's marquee event.

The Pioneers trailed Minnesota- Duluth by two goals after two periods of their national semifinal at the FleetCenter on Thursday. Despite an offense that had been ineffective and luckless to that point, a senior forward provided a voice of reason during the second intermission.

Max Bull calmly pointed out junior Luke Fulghum had scored the Pioneers' only goal to that point, and DU had entered the Frozen Four undefeated when Fulghum recorded a point. That trend continued against Minnesota-Duluth thanks to a stirring third-period rally.

The Pioneers scored four goals in the final 20 minutes to post a gritty 5-3 comeback victory, earning a berth in the national championship game Saturday against Maine (5 p.m. MDT, ESPN). The Black Bears advanced with a 2-1 victory against hometown Boston College in the other semifinal.

It will be DU's first official appearance in the final since 1969, when it won the most recent of its five national championships. The Pioneers also reached the final in 1973, although rules infractions later led the NCAA to vacate the accomplishment.

Fulghum, a Colorado Springs native, finished with a goal and an assist and senior right wing Lukas Dora scored the winning goal with 11 minutes, 35 seconds remaining.

"Max Bull, between the second and third, said, 'You know, guys, we're fine because Fulghum got his point,'" Fulghum said, referring to the Pioneers' 18-0-2 record when he records a point. "At that point, it got us going and made us believe. Stats sometimes don't lie, and that was one of the things that helped us."

Nerves and the unique talents of Minnesota-Duluth's Junior Lessard put the Pioneers in an early hole. An interference penalty on DU's Kevin Ulanski 36 seconds into the game led to a power-play goal by Lessard, the nation's leading scorer and the favorite to win the Hobey Baker Trophy as the nation's top player. Lessard deftly chipped a shot over the shoulder of DU goaltender Adam Berkhoel at 1:09, stunning a Pioneers team that watched Berkhoel pitch an impressive shutout two weeks ago against top-ranked North Dakota.

Minnesota-Duluth (28-13-4) extended the lead to 2-0 a little more than 3 minutes later on a goal by Tyler Brosz.

"When that first goal went in as early as it did, I think it took a little steam out of our sails," DU coach George Gwozdecky said. "If that hadn't gone in, I think we would have started better and would have had a better first period. You could see we didn't have the jump from that point on in the first period. We were fortunate to get out of it without too much damage."

DU (26-12-6) was outshot 11-5 in the opening period but began to turn around things in the second. A shot by Dora hit the post nearly 5 minutes into the period, but the Czech Republic native made amends about 7 minutes later. He collected the puck behind the net and centered it to Fulghum, who cut the deficit to 2-1 with his 14th goal of the season.

Lessard put the Bulldogs ahead by two goals at 15:35 with his second power-play goal, giving Minnesota-Duluth a 3-1 edge at the second intermission. Lessard could have notched a hat trick at the end of the second on a two-on-none chance against Berkhoel, but the DU goalie made the save, and the Pioneers built upon the momentum in the third.

Connor James and Ryan Caldwell scored 34 seconds apart to tie the score 3-3 with 16:56 remaining. Caldwell's goal came after Fulghum won a one-on-one possession battle with Evan Schwabe and was able to send a crossing pass to an open Caldwell.

"The first one, I maybe tried to baby it in there, so I made sure that one made the back of the net," said Caldwell, who had been stopped minutes earlier by Minnesota-Duluth goaltender Isaac Reichmuth on a similar one-on-one chance. "Lukas made a great play to Fulghum, and he really won a battle and got me the puck. I really owe those two guys."

Dora scored the winner by making a patient run between the circles and slipping a shot between Reichmuth's legs. A potential tying goal by Brosz was disallowed in the final minute after officials ruled he had charged into Berkhoel, and DU senior Greg Keith capped the scoring with an empty-net goal with 8 seconds remaining.

"The way the team responded is unbelievable," Berkhoel said. "This whole year we've been at the short end of the stick with blowing games in the third. Finally, we were able to pull one out in the third period."

A FEW GOOD DEFENSEMEN: BLUE-LINERS PROVIDE OFFENSIVE HELP TO PUT DU ON BRINK OF TITLE

Friday, April 9, 2004
By Pat Rooney
SPECIAL TO THE NEWS

Lately, when the University of Denver hockey team finds itself in need of a key goal, the Pioneers do not necessarily look to their array of talented forwards.

Often, they look back to the blue line, where hard-shooting, versatile defensemen have provided a scoring spark that has helped lead DU to the brink of its first national championship since 1969. Defensemen figured prominently in three of DU's goals Thursday in a 5-3 win against Minnesota-Duluth in the national semifinals.

The performance certainly was not an anomaly. DU blue-liners have established themselves as some of the top shooters in the NCAA tournament, which concludes Saturday when the Pioneers play for the national championship at the FleetCenter against Maine.

"It's not one or two guys - our whole defense is mobile and can get the puck to the net," sophomore defenseman Brett Skinner said. "Our coaches definitely encourage us to jump up in plays. I think it's something that has changed in the game these days. Defensemen have to be more offensive. And that is part of our team game, having the D-men jump up in plays. It obviously is a great asset for us."

Skinner got things started for DU's defensemen by launching a line drive off a faceoff early in the third period. Although Connor James was credited with the goal after tipping in the shot, Skinner's effort opened the floodgates for DU's offense.

Captain Ryan Caldwell, who created several of DU's best chances throughout the contest, tied the score 34 seconds later with his 15th goal of the season and the 26th of his career, the seventh-most goals by a defenseman in DU history. Skinner also recorded an assist on Lukas Dora's winning goal later in the third period.

"It's not just the defense. It's the forwards also recognizing that we are going to jump into the play," junior defenseman Matt Laatsch said. "We get that guy driving the middle lane, it makes it tough for the other defense.

"With Skinner's (assist), the important thing is that he got it through. When you get it through and there is traffic in front of the net, good things happen."

DU has 22 points in three NCAA tournament games, and seven have been by blue-liners. Defensemen scored all three goals in the Pioneers' 3-2 win against Miami (Ohio) in the opening round, and defensemen accounted for three of DU's 11 points Thursday.

Skinner's two assists increased his season total to 23, the third-best mark on the team, and Caldwell's 15 goals rank second behind forward Gabe Gauthier's 17. Caldwell, Skinner and freshman defenseman Matt Carle are among DU's top seven point-producers.

"One thing I think (assistant coaches) Steve Miller and Seth Appert look for in D-men is great skaters who move the puck well," Carle said. "I feel like all of us are like that. Some of us are a little bit more offensive than others, but we all try to jump up in the play when we can. When we do, good things happen. It might bite you in the butt from time to time, but more often than not you're going to get good scoring chances out of it."

Denver vs. Maine
National Championship
FleetCenter, Boston
April 10, 2004

❞Can you believe it?" Denver senior Scott McConnell wondered about an hour before the Pioneers' first appearance in the title game in 31 years. "There's two teams left, and we're one of them. Unbelievable."

Denver had finally reached The Event that Keith Magnuson had preached about. To most people, except the Pioneers themselves, it really was unbelievable that the unheralded Pioneers had reached college hockey's biggest game. No one seemed to talk about the way Maine had reached the Frozen Four - the Black Bears erased a three-goal deficit in the opening round against Harvard before defeating Wisconsin in overtime. The team that allegedly wasn't supposed to be there was Denver, which came to Boston surrounded by such phrases as "underdog," "Cinderella," and, the one little word that was most annoying to the Pioneers, "lucky."

Granted, adversity was par for the course for DU. So it was only a mild surprise when, as if their journey hadn't been bumpy enough, the Pioneers were blindsided by yet another setback hours before the faceoff against Maine.

Lukas Dora, who scored the game-winning goal against Duluth two days earlier, was suspended for the final game by Dr. M. Dianne Murphy and George Gwozdecky for a violation of team rules. Dora had recorded three points against the Bulldogs, increasing his career total to 97, and he was a prominent cog on the Pioneers' special teams. In addition to his abilities as a playmaker, Dora had played most of the season with an injured left wrist that would require surgery just days after the championship game, providing the type of grit and resiliency that sparked the Pioneers down the stretch.

Senior Lukas Dora, the team's third-leading scorer, led the semifinal win against Duluth with a goal and two assists, but he was suspended from the national championship game for a violation of team rules.

Congratulations to the
2004 National Champions
on a fantastic season!
The Burnsley Hotel
continues to be a proud
supporter of
University of Denver athletics.

Joy S. Burns

THE BURNSLEY HOTEL 1000 Grant Street, Denver, Colorado 80203, 303/830-1000
A world-class hotel and restaurant in the tradition of the fine small hotels of Europe.

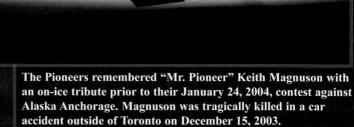

The Pioneers remembered "Mr. Pioneer" Keith Magnuson with an on-ice tribute prior to their January 24, 2004, contest against Alaska Anchorage. Magnuson was tragically killed in a car accident outside of Toronto on December 15, 2003. *Photo by Kevin Ferguson*

Senior Lukas Dora greets the media after scoring the game-winning goal in Denver's 5-3 win over Minnesota-Duluth at the Frozen Four. *Photo by Monty Rand Photography*

Frozen Four Most Outstanding Player Adam Berkhoel raises his arms in celebration of Denver's 5-3 win over Minnesota-Duluth in the national semifinals. *Photo by Monty Rand Photography*

"Toga Man" Damien Goddard and Ruckus cheer the Pioneers onto victory at the Frozen Four in Boston. Goddard has been one of Denver's proudest fans since he founded DU's Bleacher Creatures in 1986. *Photo by Rob Revitte*

Denver Pioneers – 2004 NCAA National Champions

Senior forward Greg Keith drives to the net against Maine goaltender Jimmy Howard. Keith's rugged all-around play helped Denver secure its first NCAA national championship since 1969.
Photo by Monty Rand Photography

Sophomore Gabe Gauthier, Denver's leading scorer, tallied the game-winning goal in the 1-0 victory over the University of Maine in the championship game.
Photo by Monty Rand Photography

The scoreboard at FleetCenter confirms Denver's first NCAA national championship since 1969. *Photo by Scott O'Neil*

Above: Senior captain Ryan Caldwell hoists the NCAA championship trophy moments after Denver's 1-0 win over the University of Maine.

Left: Cory Ray and Courtney Keith cheer the Pioneers onto victory at the Frozen Four.
Photos by Monty Rand Photography

Denver Pioneers - 2004 NCAA National Champions

The Pioneers celebrate their sixth NCAA national championship in school history. Denver won 11 of its last 14 games to finish the season with a 27-12-5 overall record. *Photo by Monty Rand Photography*

Assistant captain Kevin Ulanski (with trophy) and junior Jussi Halme (right) celebrate their first collegiate national championship.
Photo by Monty Rand Photography

Senior assistant captain Connor James returned to the Denver lineup just five weeks after fracturing his right fibula. James tallied the game-winning assist in the 1-0 win over the University of Maine in the Frozen Four final.
Photo by Monty Rand Photography

Denver Pioneers - 2004 NCAA National Champions

Senior Max Bull played in 154 career games at Denver. He was named to the 2004 CoSIDA Academic All-America University Division Third Team. *Photo by Monty Rand Photography*

Assistant coach Steve Miller (left), junior Nick Larson and sophomore Brett Skinner let the college hockey world know who is No. 1. *Photo by Monty Rand Photography*

Sophomore forward Ted O'Leary gives the 2004 NCAA national championship trophy a kiss. *Photo by Monty Rand Photography*

Denver Pioneers - 2004 NCAA National Champions

Senior defenseman Ryan Caldwell brings the NCAA championship trophy back to Denver on April 11, 2004. *Photo by Ken Papaleo/Rocky Mountain News*

Senior Greg Keith signs a Denver hockey jersey for one of approximately 200 fans that awaited the Pioneers' arrival from Boston back at Magness Arena in Denver. *Photo by Ken Papaleo/Rocky Mountain News*

Above: Head coach George Gwozdecky, who became the first individual to win NCAA titles as a player (Wisconsin '77), assistant coach (Michigan State '86) and head coach (Denver '04) greets over 2,500 fans at a Welcome Home Rally at Magness Arena. *Photo by University of Denver Media Relations*

Below: Diane Wendt (left) and Joy Burns (right) celebrate the Pioneers' NCAA national championship at the Welcome Home Rally. Wendt was a longtime DU athletics administrator and is a member of the school's Athletics Hall of Fame. Burns, who is the chair of Denver's Board of Trustees, has been one of the University of Denver's most loyal supporters. *Photo by University of Denver Media Relations*

Above: The Pioneers received a special senate resolution at the state capital building in downtown Denver on April 16. The Pioneers were guests of Colorado state senator John Evans of district 30 and the 64th general assembly of the state of Colorado. *Photo by University of Denver Media Relations*

Denver Pioneers - 2004 NCAA National Champions

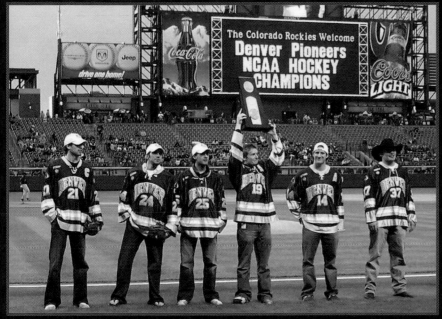

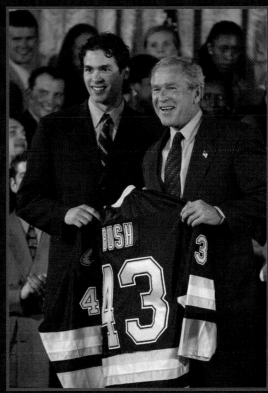

Left: Connor James (with trophy) and the rest of the senior class were special guest of the Colorado Rockies on April 14, 2004. Senior Ryan Caldwell, Adam Berkhoel, Greg Keith, Max Bull and Scott McConnell join James on the field prior to the game.
Photo by University of Denver Media Relations

Captain Ryan Caldwell presents President George W. Bush a Denver hockey jersey at the team's visit to the White House on May 19, 2004. The Pioneers were guests of the President on "Champions Day."
Photo by The White House

Above: The Pioneers were honored by the Colorado Avalanche during their playoff game against the Dallas Stars. *Photo by Tim De Frisco/De Frisco Photography*

The DU hockey senior class of 2004 (Front, L-R: Lukas Dora, Scott McConnell, Adam Berkhoel and Max Bull; Back, L-R: Connor James, Ryan Caldwell and Greg Keith) posted 99 wins in four years.
Photo by University of Denver Media Relations

Colorado Rockies manager Clint Hurdle presented head coach George Gwozdecky with a home jersey prior to their game against the Arizona Diamondbacks.
Photo by University of Denver Media Relations

Denver Pioneers - 2004 NCAA National Champions

CONGRATULATIONS TO THE

PIONEERS

FSN
FOX SPORTS NET™

HOME OF THE DENVER PIONEERS HOCKEY TEAM

CATCH PIONEER HOCKEY ON FOX SPORTS NET
AND THE ROCKY MOUNTAIN SPORTS REPORT

ROCKY MOUNTAIN
Sports Report

Dora was one of DU's emotional leaders. Gwozdecky described the senior's style of play as similar to the chaotic whirlwind left in the cartoon wake of the Tasmanian Devil, wrecking havoc all over the ice in a maniacal blur. Dora might make a critical turnover one night, then take it upon himself to turn in a multi-point game the following night. He was one of the team's biggest hitters, and his bilingual trash-talking was a constant nuisance to DU's opponents.

Obviously, it was a gut-wrenching decision for Denver's administration. But at a private school where integrity and character are standard for student-athletes, doing the right thing was par for the course.

"When we made the decision that one of our key players was not going to play, I really thought we were committing suicide," Chancellor Dan Ritchie said. "One less talented player can make the difference in a tight game. You

Chancellor Daniel L. Ritchie thought the Pioneers showed great character in overcoming the suspension of senior Lukas Dora for the national championship game.

knew it was not going to help things. He had just made the winning goal in the Duluth game and you know he had a passion for it."

Despite spending much of the afternoon trying to talk Gwozdecky out of his decision, Dora accepted his punishment with class, becoming the Pioneers' top cheerleader during the thrilling finale. Ironically, the superstitious Dora asked his parents to remain home in his native Czech Republic because, years earlier, his junior team lost every time mom and dad visited. At least they didn't have to watch their son watch the game from the stands.

"It's the policy. I broke it, so I don't play," Dora said. "I love coach. He made me the player I am. I appreciate everything he has done in my life the past four years. People make mistakes in life, and I paid for it."

Yet by this time the Pioneers had overcome so much adversity that losing their third-leading scorer hardly seemed like a hurdle at all. The Pioneers were touched by the voracious crowd that lined up outside their hotel to cheer as the team departed for the FleetCenter. Plus Denver could bank on Berkhoel, a goalie who already had a national championship on his resume. It was a fitting situation for a netminder who had been defying expectations since he laced up his first pair of skates.

Tina Berkhoel, Adam's mother, was a fixture during the national telecast of the final, wincing and covering her face each time her 22-year old son turned away another Maine salvo. It was a far cry from the parent who was ambivalent about her son's infatuation with hockey as a youngster.

"My parents didn't really want me to play hockey at the start," said Berkhoel, who was an eighth-round selection of the NHL's Chicago Blackhawks in 2000. "Then they said I couldn't play goalie and I couldn't travel. I started playing hockey and loved the game. I wanted to be a goalie. I thought it would be fun to do."

Before coming to Denver, goaltender Adam Berkhoel won a Junior A national championship with the Twin Cities Vulcans, impressing the DU coaching staff with his fiery competitive drive.

Recruiters weren't exactly salivating over Berkhoel, and he was stung by the lack of interest from any of his homestate schools in Minnesota. Assistant coach Steve Miller was a college teammate of one of Berkhoel's high school coaches, Scott Faust, and when Denver first started to look at Berkhoel, Faust promised Miller that, "If Adam doesn't make it, it won't be from lack of effort."

Focused and determined, the unheralded Berkhoel carried a chip on his shoulder when he took his game to the Twin Cities Vulcans of the United States Hockey League. There he quickly earned a reputation for producing in big games, earning a spot in the USHL's All-Star game by posting a .923 saves percentage and a 2.72 goals-against average.

Berkhoel led the Vulcans to an unexpected USA Junior A National Championship, which paved the way for his selection by the Blackhawks. It also encouraged Gwozdecky, who had listened to assistant coach Seth Appert rave endlessly about Berkhoel's potential. Despite Appert's confidence, Denver was recruiting Berkhoel as a walk-on, believing they would offer a scholarship to a more highly-touted goalie prospect the following year.

"I went to watch him, and right away I noticed his athleticism as a goalie," Appert said. "But the biggest thing we liked was his competitive nature. He was always battling to make saves. Combine that with his athleticism, and his style was different. It wasn't maybe as refined as it needed to be, but we were really impressed with what he had."

Berkhoel's performance for the Vulcans during the postseason made Denver believe it was getting a better player than expected. It also sparked late interest in Berkhoel from the University of Minnesota. Since Berkhoel was being recruited as a walk-on he couldn't sign a letter of intent for DU, opening the door for Minnesota or any other school that wanted to toss a scholarship his way. Yet Berkhoel stuck to his verbal commitment to Denver, and a twist of fate allowed him to receive a scholarship after all when Mark Rycroft left DU following the 2000 season to sign an NHL contract with the St. Louis Blues.

Berkhoel shared the starting role for two seasons with Wade Dubielewicz but came into his own in 2003-2004, tying Denver's single-season record with seven shutouts.

"We knew we had a good kid to see so much character in a young man," Appert said. "When he [honored his verbal commitment], it really showed the kind of person he is. I don't know too many kids from Minnesota who would make that choice."

At Denver, however, Berkhoel had to patiently wait in the shadows of Wade Dubielewicz. Though Gwozdecky always lumped the pair together - often referring to his goalies as No. 1 and No. 1A - it was Berkhoel who was saddled with the "A" beside his billing.

Berkhoel appeared in 15 games as a freshman, posting a record of 7-5-1, and during his sophomore season he began alternating starts regularly with Dubielewicz. While Berkhoel posted an impressive .917 saves percentage during DU's dominant 2001-02 season, Dubielewicz became only the fourth Pioneers player to be nominated for the Hobey Baker award by leading the nation with a .943 saves percentage and posting a paltry goals-against average of 1.72. Both numbers are the best single-season marks in DU hockey history.

Berkhoel lowered his goals-against average to 2.30 during his junior year while notching three shutouts. But Dubielewicz one-upped him again, posting a better saves percentage (.912 to .908) and earning second team All-WCHA honors.

Their competition was as fierce as it was amiable. Still good friends, Berkhoel often credits Dubielewicz's presence as a key factor in his development. Dubielewicz, who enjoyed a record-setting rookie season with the Bridgeport Sound Tigers of the American Hockey League, took as much pleasure watching Berkhoel pass him on many of DU's career charts as he did notching his first NHL win in the spring of 2004.

"What Adam did down the stretch was give the guys confidence," Dubielewicz said. "It was great to see how far he had come in the last few years. It was a big thing this year to see if he could take the reins and shoulder the load. Obviously he stepped up to the plate and hit a home run."

Between his championship experience with the Twin Cities Vulcans and his time training with Dubielewicz, Berkhoel developed a keen eye for how national championship teams are pieced together. As he watched Maine

defeat Boston College in the Frozen Four semifinals, Berkhoel had a realization. If he and Maine goaltender Jimmy Howard canceled each other out in the expected battle of goalies, it was his Pioneers that held the overall edge.

"We watched them, and the reason they were at the championship game was because of Jimmy Howard," Berkhoel said. "All you heard about was their goaltending. For us, we did it with a total team effort. That's where we had the advantage. We weren't basing our game plan on one particular guy. We had the whole team that got us there. We didn't change anything up just to beat them. We just didn't want to beat ourselves."

Dora was replaced by Ted O'Leary, a sophomore from suburban Arvada who had filled in admirably for James while he recovered from his fractured leg. Much like the semifinal against Minnesota-Duluth, the Pioneers stood tall during an emotional opening burst by Maine. They also benefited from what many players believed was a helping hand from their spiritual seventh skater, Keith Magnuson. The Pioneers had finally reached The Event; Magnuson's spirit would influence them on the ice as much as he did during his

Super sub Ted O'Leary, who replaced the injured Connor James for four games, substituted for Lukas Dora in the national championship game and anchored Denver's young fourth line.

fiery, influential visit to the DU locker room six long months earlier.

It turned out the Pioneers would need any edge they could get, spiritual or otherwise. A penalty on Max Bull gave the Black Bears a power play chance less than four minutes into the contest. Maine appeared to score the all-important first goal moments later when a patient Derek Damon pushed a shot past Berkhoel. But a video review revealed that the skate of Maine's Mike Hamilton had inched into the crease. Although Hamilton never touched Berkhoel, the goal was disallowed.

The sudden momentum shift was debilitating for Maine, since Hamilton's wayward toe had absolutely no effect on Berkhoel or the play. But a rule is a rule, and the abrupt twist of fate stirred the hearts of DU's fans.

"All of us old guys were standing there wondering 'Was that Magnuson's hand that went down there and pushed the skate in the crease?'" said Gerry Powers, Magnuson's former teammate who was the goaltender for DU's championship teams of 1968 and 1969.

Powers was just one of countless DU hockey alums attending the game, and their spines tingled again following another inexplicable play midway through the second period. Maine junior Ben Murphy took advantage of a line change after a long shift to set up a breakaway chance against Berkhoel. But Denver's goalie was let off the hook when Murphy seemingly tripped over nothing. The obvious explanation was that Murphy had lost an edge on his skate, or perhaps simply lost his balance. Many of the Pioneers had a different explanation. They believed a subtle hip-check had been delivered by the most rugged guardian angel in hockey history.

"Me and Berkie looked at each other when that happened and said, 'Maggie tripped him.' No one was even around the guy," Greg Keith said. "It was like having a seventh guy on the ice. No one really talked about it, but there definitely was an aura."

Gwozdecky also believed that Magnuson had delivered a phantom check, and Maine's missed opportunities allowed Denver to take advantage of a power play situation and strike first. Working on a power play near the midpoint of the first period, Connor James, his broken leg now long forgotten, jostled for the puck along the back wall before winning a possession battle with Maine's Troy Barnes deep in the left corner. The final assist of James' career would also be his biggest, as the left wing slid a pass to an open Gabe Gauthier camped in the left slot.

Known more for speed than brawn, senior Connor James outworked two Maine defenders to win the puck and slide a perfect game-winning assist to Gabe Gauthier in the first period of the national championship game.

Monty Rand Photography

Known more for his speed than his brawn, the 5-foot-11, 185-pound James beat two bigger Maine skaters to deliver the puck to Gauthier.

"We were on the power play, and a big reason why our power play wasn't working was that when we lost the puck, we weren't hunting it down. We weren't going after it," James said. "A big part of that play was Caldwell. He was down low with me and helped free the puck. I gave a quick look and saw Gabe in the slot and fired it over."

Gauthier had meticulously done his homework on Howard during the semifinals and the sophomore center picked his spot accordingly, calmly tucking a low shot under Howard's right side to give the Pioneers the lead. It was Gauthier's 18th goal of the year and his eighth tally on the power play, both of which led the team.

"I knew by watching them in the semifinals that Howard had a quick glove," Gauthier said. "I told the guys to stay away from his glove. Connor made that great play, pushing off a guy that was twice his size. I was hollering like a lone ranger in front of the net. He threw me the puck, and I kept it low like I knew we should."

Gauthier's goal was all Berkhoel and his defensemen would need, but in typical fashion for a team that did nothing the easy way all season long, Denver would have to survive some of the most heart-pounding final minutes in the 57-year history of the national championship game.

Through two periods Maine owned a 15-10 advantage in shots. The Black Bears were scoreless in four power play opportunities, including three in the first period, thanks to Berkhoel and a team-wide commitment to blocking Maine's chances, regardless of how many bruises it caused.

Time after time Pioneers skaters sprawled their bodies across the ice to block Maine shots. It was a source of continued frustration for Maine, which finished with a 24-20 shot advantage but had some of its best looks smothered by the selfless Pioneers.

The Pioneers blocked an eye-popping 27 shots in the final.

"Once we got that lead, we didn't know if we would win with one goal, but we wanted to play smart," Luke Fulghum said. "We wanted to get the puck out of the danger zone and continue to play our smart, defensive game like we'd been playing."

Denver increased its pressure in the third period, producing a 10-9 shot advantage in the final frame. But Howard turned away every Pioneers chance, setting up the furious finish.

Sophomore Gabe Gauthier capped his breakout season with the only goal of the title game, a power-play tally midway through the first period. Gauthier led the team in goals (18), power-play goals (8), and game-winning goals (6).

Still clinging to the one-goal lead, the chaotic conclusion began when Matt Laatsch was whistled for a hooking penalty with 2:09 remaining. Maine's power play had been punchless to that point, but a rare lapse of composure by Denver moments later would give the Black Bears an improbable opportunity.

Gauthier, desperate to clear the puck, gloved a Maine pass and tried to shovel it out of the Denver zone. Referee Tim Kotyra correctly called a delay of game penalty, giving the Black Bears a 5-on-3 opportunity with 1:34 remaining. Gauthier and Laatsch watched anxiously from the box as Maine coach Tim Whitehead pulled Howard about 20 seconds later, giving Maine a 6-on-3 advantage in its desperate quest for a tying goal.

Denver's fans braced for the attack, screaming from their corner that loomed over Berkhoel's crease. University of Denver Chancellor Daniel Ritchie already was reassuring himself that the Pioneers would prevail in overtime. Dora and McConnell suffered together in the corner of the stands, their neckties getting tighter and tighter, unable to watch yet unable to turn away. In Pennsylvania, Dubielewicz had just pitched his ninth shutout of the year for Bridgeport, setting the American Hockey League record for shutouts as a rookie. As his coach berated the team for its scoreless tie, Dubielewicz's eyes were focused on the guys in the training room flashing him hand signals about Maine's desperate power play.

A hooking penalty on junior Matt Laatsch gave Maine a power play chance with 2:09 remaining. A penalty on Gabe Gauthier 35 seconds later gave the Black Bears a two-man advantage, which Maine increased to a 6-on-3 when goalie Jimmy Howard was pulled with about 78 seconds remaining.

Maine's fans came to life, since the tying goal surely was just a shot or two away. About the only people in the FleetCenter not unnerved by the situation were the ones on the Pioneers' bench. Most of them found it fitting. Nothing had been done the easy way all season; naturally, the season's final 75 seconds would be the toughest test yet.

Gwozdecky looked over his troops and told them with all the confidence and sincerity in the world that they would get through this together. He reminded everyone that they had weathered too much adversity to let a little 6-on-3 disadvantage rattle them. Gwozdecky selected Ryan Caldwell, Greg Keith, Matt Carle and Max Bull to share the responsibility of keeping the six Black Bears from reaching the net. As he had all year, Caldwell kept making jokes with Gwozdecky and his teammates along the bench during what should have been nerve-racking timeouts.

"It was fitting we had to win it that way. Nothing has been handed to us easy this year," said the captain, who had insisted he be a part of the final penalty kill. "I thought maybe if I could show that I wasn't uptight that maybe the other guys would see that and relax. I didn't want to let the guys know that any of us were nervous and that we were going to get it done."

Caldwell's unflappable wit helped break the tension and turned an impossible task into a simple game of time management.

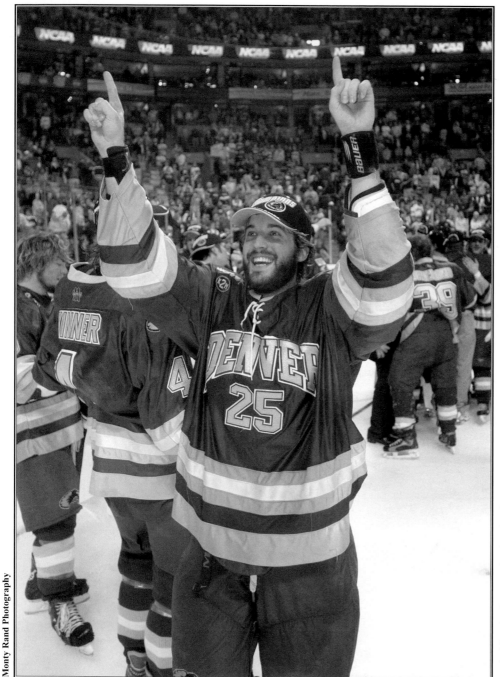

Senior Greg Keith, who played the point among DU's three penalty killers during the heart-pounding finale, celebrates his championship effort.

"We were just trying to watch the clock," Carle said. "It was so hectic out there. They just kept firing pucks. We were trying to let Berkie be able to see them, because we know if he sees them he's definitely going to make the save."

Berkhoel made several saves during the sequence, but he was aided by some jittery puck-handling by Maine. An errant pass between Maine defensemen allowed the puck to escape DU's zone once, and most of the Black Bears' heaviest shots were off target.

Berkhoel snatched one shot out of the air with about 40 seconds remaining. Winded and frantic, Berkhoel wanted to call a timeout. In his final on-ice directive as the captain, Caldwell vetoed his goalie's request.

"They had a couple good opportunities, but they never had that great back-door play or anything like that," Berkhoel said of the exhausting final minute. "With that last whistle with 40 seconds left, I wanted a timeout, but Ryan called me off because he knew their first unit was off the ice. I didn't realize that. I was just dying out there from moving around. But I felt after we killed the first little bit that we had a chance. We cleared the zone once and I felt they would only get a couple more chances. They never really got anything in tight. We blocked all the shots from the outside."

Gwozdecky used the quick break to substitute Max Bull for Keith, whose knees were quivering after chasing the puck around the perimeter as the point-man of Denver's three penalty killers.

"I remember just laying on the ice exhausted, but if it was anyone else but Bull coming in I would have tried to stay out there," Keith said. "I knew Bully had as much confidence as anyone."

Maine's final shot whistled high and wide, caroming around the left corner. None of the six Black Bears could get a stick on the puck, which slid slowly to the other end of the ice as the final seconds ticked away. Laatsch, released from the box for a two-minute penalty that seemed to last an eternity, chased the puck toward the empty net, but the effort wasn't necessary. Gloves and helmets began to arc through the air from the DU bench as the jubilant players spilled on to the ice.

The Journey finally was over. The Event conquered. The Team had won the championship for the first time since 1969 with an effort that exemplified the power of having 27 players sacrificing their bodies, time, and personal interests for the sake of the group. As Magnuson would always say, for the sake of The Team.

The Pioneers swarmed Berkhoel's crease, right in front of the ecstatic corner of the FleetCenter packed with wild-eyed DU fans. After protecting his net in miserly fashion, recording two 1-0 shutouts in his final three games, Berkhoel gladly allowed his teammates to celebrate in his sanctuary. No one wanted to leave.

"I think the celebration took longer than our game," Berkhoel said. "They had to kick us off the ice. We wanted to capture every moment and be together as long as we could. Everyone felt that being together for one last time was pretty special. We wanted to stay out there one last time and capture everything we had."

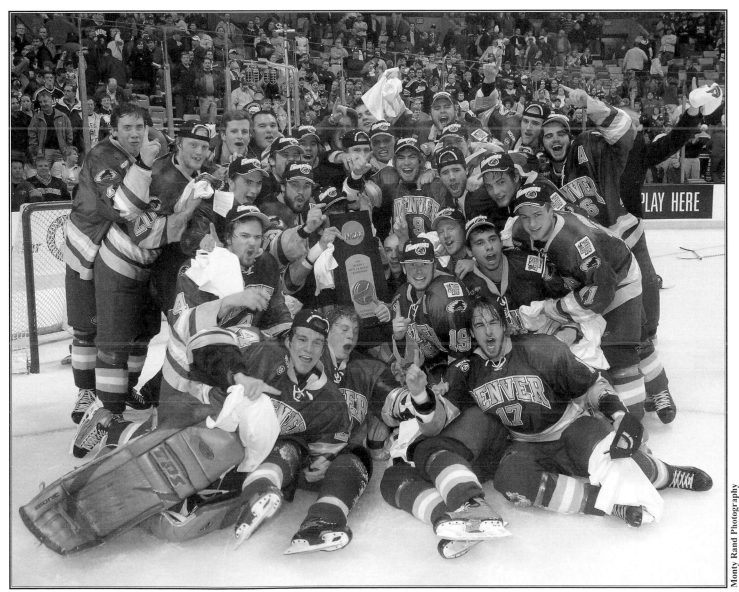

Monty Rand Photography

DU's 1-0 victory secured the school's sixth national championship and its first since 1969. With The Event conquered and The Journey finally complete, The Team didn't want to leave the giddy scene on the ice at the FleetCenter.

The victory secured the sixth national championship in Denver's illustrious history, its first in 35 years. Fans poured out of apartments and bars near campus to celebrate. Back in Boston the team began a victory party that stretched through the ensuing weeks and also captured the imagination of the team's forefathers in the Denver program.

"This is a situation we've all been waiting for," Powers said. "This school has too much tradition, too much hockey history. We've had a lot of great hockey players, a lot of great teams that couldn't win a national championship. For a while you wondered if they would ever be able to do it again. For these kids to do this is so awesome."

The DU locker room swirled with smiles and laughter. Berkhoel, who had just been named the Frozen Four's Most Outstanding Player, calmly deflected praise for his accomplishment toward his defensemen. Dora graciously explained his affection toward Gwozdecky and his lack of enmity over his suspension, secure in the (correct) knowledge that his contribution to the national championship was as important as anyone's. Matt Carle tried unsuccessfully to articulate how it felt to become the first American to win a gold medal at the World Junior Championships and capture an NCAA title in the same season. Along one wall a tearful Adrian Veideman snuggled with the trophy, his face a mask of overpowering joy and complete emotional fatigue.

Chancellor Ritchie visited the raucous DU locker room to find a team transformed. The Pioneers were on the cusp of greatness when Ritchie visited the locker room following their victory in the West Regional final against North Dakota, a win that accelerated the curve of their fledging confidence and willpower. Now they officially were champions.

"I'll never forget it as long as I live. The faces of the players, you can't describe it in words," Ritchie said. "The glow, it was like different people almost. The joy, the thrill, the rush…how can you describe it? You can't. I've been in locker rooms before, but I had never seen faces like those. The cheers when I walked into the room, I had never heard anything that loud before. It was an emotional thing for me as well. I think I told them the ring factory would have to put in some extra work."

The Pioneers come together one last time to sing the team's fight song before taking the party into the locker room.

Rocky Mountain News

DU'S GAUTHIER FINDS BACK OF NET, CONFIDENCE

Wednesday, April 7, 2004
By Pat Rooney
SPECIAL TO THE NEWS

Like most players, Gabe Gauthier had a list of goals when the University of Denver hockey team began practice in late September.

As a sophomore with a full year of college hockey experience, the Buena Park, Calif., native expected to improve on his rookie season. What Gauthier didn't expect was to be the leading scorer on a team headed to the Frozen Four.

Gauthier will be the focus of DU's offense when the Pioneers face Western Collegiate Hockey Association rival Minnesota-Duluth in the NCAA semifinals Thursday at Boston (10 a.m. MDT, ESPN2), a situation that seemed like an impossible dream for a player who produced only eight goals and eight assists as a freshman.

"I took a look at last year and how I played, and I knew I could play better," Gauthier said. "I just needed that confidence. Last year, I focused on the defensive game instead of how I know to play, and that is offensively. Now, I just focus on playing my game and playing consistent."

Gauthier will take a team-leading 42 points into the Frozen Four, where DU hopes the sophomore center can continue his penchant for recording key points. Gauthier is tied for the team lead with seven power-play goals, and 13 of his team-leading 25 assists have come while the Pioneers have had a man advantage.

Gauthier leads the Pioneers with five winning goals and he helped lead the offense when it struggled with inconsistency during the first half of the season. Gauthier put together a stretch of nine games in November in which he collected multiple points six times. His career-best eight-game points-scoring streak was halted during the Pioneers' 1-0 win against North Dakota in the West Regional final March 27.

"When we recruited him, we expected him to be a major contributor as a freshman, and I know he probably was more disappointed than anybody that he wasn't able to contribute as expected," DU coach George Gwozdecky said. "There is no question that his development, and his taking responsibility for what he needs to do a better job of, all have made him the kind of player we expected him to be.

"His academics and understanding of what he had to do at the university is more directed. He trained a lot harder and came into camp in great shape. Those two things really allowed him to come out of the gate and play the way he is capable of."

Gauthier will look to get back into the scoring column against Duluth, which might face the reunion of the potent Connor James-Gauthier-Lukas Dora line that led DU for much of the season. James is hoping to play for the first time since breaking his right fibula against Colorado College on March 5, although his ice time and effectiveness likely will be limited.

Gauthier credited his pairing with the two senior wings for alleviating some of the pressure on him until his confidence took hold early in the season.

"I had a lot of help from the guys I was playing with," he said. "I started with Dora and Connor, and we really racked up the points. It just kept getting better for me. I had confidence in myself to start doing the things I had in the past."

The Pioneers counted their blessings in every conceivable way. They credited each other for the inner resolve and persistence that allowed them to overcome their midseason woes. They thanked their coaching staff for the balance they provided, cajoling and tinkering with the team when things were bad, then prodding them to relax and be themselves as the team began to roll. And they gave props to Keith Magnuson, their seventh skater who accompanied them on this Journey to the very end, all the way through the Event he promised them they would conquer.

"We had a great friend of the Pioneer program pass away, and that was a blow because he was such a great inspiration to a lot of us seniors," Greg Keith said. "Right now, I guarantee one thing: He's smiling down and he's a happy man."

The party eventually progressed to the team hotel, where a hastily planned reception turned into a rambunctious victory party. The Pioneers were greeted by their families, friends, alumni, and fans. Most were still stunned and speechless about the improbable ending to an improbable season. Most of the parents were savoring well-deserved sighs of relief. All except one, anyway.

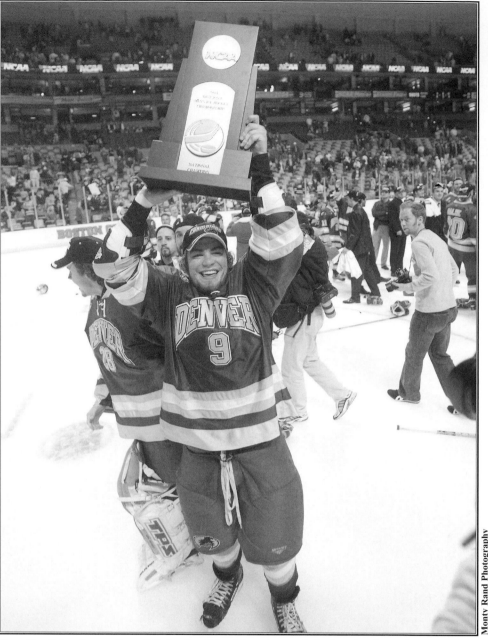

Pam Gauthier, the mother of Gabe Gauthier (above), revealed after the championship victory that she had been heartened two days earlier by the lottery-like luck of the numbers that directed her to her seat at the FleetCenter.

Pam Gauthier, the proud mother of Gabe Gauthier, had been keeping a secret. For days she kept it from her son for fear of jinxing the charm. At the postgame reception, Pam Gauthier explained to Gabe how she was confident Denver would prevail from the moment she picked up her Frozen Four tickets two days earlier. She had to rub her eyes after seeing the numbers that indicated her seat. She would watch the entire Frozen Four in Section 4 (the age Gabe started playing hockey), Row 16 (the number of years Gabe had been playing hockey), Seat 9 (his jersey number).

The numbers felt luckier than those of a lottery winner. Immediately Pam Gauthier was brimming with faith. It's no wonder her son scored the only goal in the championship game.

"When she got the tickets she looked at them and put it together, she had a feeling we would win the whole thing," Gabe Gauthier said. "Of course she didn't tell me until the reception afterward. It's probably better that I didn't know."

It was impossible for many to keep the tears from flowing, whether it was the emotionally invested parents or the avid fans of college hockey. Denver had overcome so much to get to this point - standing with friends and family at the pinnacle of triumph, hoisting celebratory toasts - that the enormity of what they had accomplished was impossible to process. No one had ever doubted the Pioneers' talent. But to put it all together after the dreary depths of winter, a time when they were grieving for Magnuson and struggling just to win a game at home, made the championship incalculably more stirring.

"This experience is so much different than if we would have won two years ago with that great team we had," Gwozdecky said. "That would have been great, but we were the No. 1 team from January on. We were the No. 1 seed in the West Regional. To win it would have been a relief more than anything else. This year we were clawing and gouging to keep our heads above water. We had to fight externally and internally. To come back and turn the college hockey world on its ear, it's a special story."

So special that it touched almost everyone who followed the Pioneers. Seeing the utter joy on the players' faces, sensing the relief in their eyes that their sacrifices, faith, and commitment had paid off in such glorious fashion, couldn't help but impress any observer.

The Pioneers from the University of Denver once again were the kings of college hockey. The Journey, as defined by Keith Magnuson, was carrying the championship trophy back to Denver.

"Seeing the coaches' faces, the joy they had, was such a special thing," Dr. M. Dianne Murphy said. "Knowing how hard it is for anybody to win a national championship, the pinnacle of what it means to say you're the best at that one particular thing…it was a combination of relief and joy and happiness, and a culmination of hard work. I was so emotional about it, and I'm not considered a real emotional person, I just cried. I was so happy for those young men and George and the coaches. And knowing in your own mind that we did it the right way. That is something they will never forget."

Susie Coombe, John Coombe, Dr. M. Dianne Murphy, Dan Van Ackeren, Pam Wettig and Stu Halsall cheer the Pioneers onto victory at the Frozen Four.

Rocky Mountain News

DU WINS FIRST HOCKEY TITLE SINCE 1969

Saturday, April 10, 2004
By Pat Rooney
SPECIAL TO THE NEWS

BOSTON - University of Denver coach George Gwozdecky has been steadfast in his opinion that Adam Berkhoel is the best goaltender in the nation.

Of course, a boast like that is easily debatable. But during the national championship game on Saturday at the FleetCenter, Berkhoel proved his coach was right all along. And because of his efforts, the championship trophy finally is coming back to Denver.

Berkhoel completed his dominance of the NCAA tournament against Maine, leading the Pioneers to a 1-0 victory to give DU its sixth national championship and its first since 1969. Berkhoel notched his second 1-0 shutout in three games and produced only the third shutout in the 57-year history of the national championship game.

Sophomore Gabe Gauthier scored the Pioneers' lone goal at the 12 minute, 26 second mark of the first period, and Berkhoel did the rest. The senior from Woodbury, Minn., made 24 saves and kept the Black Bears from scoring during an exhausting 6-on-3 situation in the final 1:15.

"I knew I had to come out and keep Maine off the board for as long as I could," Berkhoel said. "I felt like we had the hockey Gods on our side."

It is fitting that Berkhoel mentioned divine powers in his description of DU's championship, since there is plenty of evidence that the Pioneers were a team of destiny.

Former DU standout Keith Magnuson, who remained close to the program throughout his life, died in a car accident in December, and it certainly seemed as if someone was looking over the team in the championship game. Gwozdecky suspended Lukas Dora, the team's third-leading scorer, for a violation of team rules on Saturday morning, yet sophomore Ted O'Leary, a native of Arvada, filled Dora's spot in the lineup and helped anchor the Pioneers' fourth line.

Maine also appeared to put DU on its heels with a goal by Derek Damon just over 5 minutes into the contest, but the replay officials ruled that Mike Hamilton was in the crease, and the goal was disallowed.

"It looked like he was in the crease, and the fact that they reviewed it and called it off was a big boost for us," defenseman Ryan Caldwell said. "Getting first goals was a key for us all season. We did that and rode it to the win."

Gauthier's goal, his team-leading 18th of the season, came on a power play opportunity. Left wing Connor James won a possession battle in the corner and sent a pinpoint crossing pass to an open Gauthier on the right side. Gauthier had Maine goalie Jimmy Howard scouted perfectly, making sure he stayed away from Howard's glove side by tucking a low shot past the sophomore goaltender's stick.

"I knew by watching them against Boston College (in the semifinals) that he had a quick glove. I told the guys to stay away from his glove," said Gauthier, who ended the season as DU's scoring leader with 43 points. "Connor made that great play, pushing off a guy that was twice his size. I was hollering like a lone ranger in front of the net. He threw me the puck, and I kept it low like I knew we should."

It was an emotional effort by James, a senior who rejoined the lineup at the Frozen Four for the first time since breaking his right fibula on March 5. James promised his teammates that if they made it to Boston he would be ready to play, and he responded by recording a goal and two assists in the two games.

James earned a spot on the All-Tournament team with Caldwell and Berkhoel, who also was named the tournament's Most Outstanding Player.

"To end my career like this, words can't describe it," James said. "The coaches could see I was more comfortable (Saturday) than I was on Thursday."

Yet before the Pioneers could celebrate, they had to watch Berkhoel withstand a final barrage by a Maine team that boasted twice as many skaters in the final 75 seconds. Junior defenseman Matt Laatsch was called for a hooking penalty with 2:09 remaining, and he was joined in the box 35 seconds later by Gauthier, who was whistled for a delay of game violation.

Maine, which went 0-for-6 on the power play, pulled Howard with 1:15 left in order to press the Pioneers with a 6-on-3 advantage. But Berkhoel held strong, making several deft saves while the trio of Caldwell, Matt Carle, and Greg Keith kept the six Black Bears at bay.

"We haven't done anything easy all year," Keith said. "Everything we do, we wind up doing it the hard way. This is a close group of guys that know we can overcome any challenge, and that is what brought us the national championship."

UNBELIEVABLE JOURNEY NOW REALITY FOR DU; CARLE INSTRUMENTAL AS PIONEERS WIN FIRST CROWN IN 35 YEARS

Monday, April 12, 2004
By Pat Rooney
SPECIAL TO THE NEWS

BOSTON - Matt Carle really wanted someone to pinch him.

Not surprisingly, Carle's unusual request amid a rambunctious locker room went unfulfilled. But even if his wish had been granted, the University of Denver's freshman defenseman was not going to suddenly find himself in a less triumphant reality.

Truth is, Carle is the only player in the country who has collected trophies at two of hockey's most prestigious events this season-the World Junior Championships and the NCAA Frozen Four.

DU's legendary program finally returned to national prominence Saturday as the Pioneers earned their first national championship in 35 years with a thrilling 1-0 victory against Maine at the FleetCenter.

Carle, who missed 14 games this season because of an ankle injury and his call-up to the World Junior team, was a fixture on DU's blue line and also was a key contributor to the United States' first gold medal at the World Juniors in January.

"They are incomparable," Carle said. "This is good, because I've been with these guys all year long. But at the same time, the World Juniors was good because I knew a bunch of those guys, too. They were both great experiences. I guess the only way it could get better than this would be to win a Stanley Cup."

Carle finished the year as the top-scoring freshman on the team, posting 26 points while ranking fifth on the team with 21 assists. He was a steadying force along the blue line, and head coach George Gwozdecky did not hesitate to rely on the talented rookie during the spine-tingling final moments of the championship game.

Two DU penalties gave Maine a late five-on-three advantage, which, the Black Bears increased to a six-on-three situation after pulling goalie Jimmy Howard with 1 minute, 15 seconds remaining.

Carle was one of the Pioneers' three penalty killers, along with seniors Greg Keith and Ryan Caldwell, during the wild finish.

The trio was able to keep Maine off the scoreboard long enough to collect the program's sixth national championship, its first since winning consecutive titles in 1968 and 969.

"We were just trying to watch the clock. That's pretty much all we were doing," Carle said. "It was hectic out there. (Maine) kept firing pucks, and we just tried to let (goalie Adam Berkhoel) see them, because we knew if he did, he would make the save."

TOUGH DEBUT: It's tough to find a young athlete who doesn't dream of making the highlight reel of ESPN's Sportscenter. But junior defenseman Matt Laatsch might not want to remember his national highlight debut.

The image of Laatsch holding his head in his hands in the penalty box during Maine's late power play aired repeatedly Saturday night. Laatsch was released in time to join the celebration after his teammates cleared the puck one last time.

"I was praying in the box," Laatsch said. "I got out with 11 seconds or so left, and right after that the celebration started.

I was this close to being the goat taking that penalty, and then you go from one end of the spectrum to the other."

Epilogue

William R. Sallaz

Connor James, Matt Laatsch and Nick Larson share a laugh on the ice at the FleetCenter shortly after DU captured its first national championship in 35 years.

For Connor James the amazing Journey started to wind down just like it began, floating across America on an airplane bound for Denver.

Over eight months earlier James flew to Denver to help at Coach Gwozdecky's summer hockey camp. Back then he wondered what would happen during his upcoming senior season. Never in his wildest dreams did he imagine this: Resting on the seat between James and Max Bull was the national championship trophy, nestled comfortably with its own pillow and blanket.

The Pioneers celebrated throughout the night in Boston, but fatigue finally caught up with them as soon as they hit their seats for the giddy trip back home. The flight provided the last chance for sleep for the players for weeks to come.

Somewhere amid all the gentle snores and pleasant dreams, a wide-awake George Gwozdecky sat with his wife Bonnie. Physically, DU's coach was as sleep-deprived as everyone else. Mentally and emotionally, however, Gwozdecky was alert and wistful. He had just become the first person in the history of college hockey to win a national championship as a player (at Wisconsin, 1977), an assistant coach (at Michigan State, 1986), and as a head coach. Yet this dizzying accomplishment was the furthest thing from his mind. Instead George and Bonnie were reminiscing about their lives together, personally as well as in hockey. They met while Gwozdecky was at Michigan State, and now it seemed as if every step along their own personal journey had led to this moment. This Event.

"It was kind of surreal. We both had this silly little smile on our faces," he recalled. "I knew three hours from now, something would happen to disrupt my tranquillity. Yet that moment was so pleasant. I've never experienced that before. Of all the times we've had since we won, that's been the one point I recall with a great amount of affection."

Gwozdecky was right on two counts - his tranquillity was about to be pleasantly shattered, and there would be many "times" to share in the ensuing celebration.

Crimson & Gold: The Denver Pioneers' Magical Run to the 2004 National Championship ═══════════ **89**

The jubilant Pioneers needed every minute of the sleep they enjoyed on the plane, because they hit the ground running when they landed in Denver on Sunday morning. A modest crowd greeted their return to campus, but the somewhat small turnout really wasn't so surprising; their most faithful fans were either still in Boston or were easing through a slow Sunday morning after the celebrations of the preceding night.

No matter. Most of the seniors piled into Greg Keith's Hummer and woke the school by tearing around campus, a scraggly Ryan Caldwell raising the trophy triumphantly through the sunroof. In many ways the ride didn't stop for weeks.

The outpouring of affection and congratulations overwhelmed everyone surrounding the team, from the players to the coaching staff and administration and even to Chancellor Daniel L. Ritchie. Gwozdecky was inundated with over a thousand emails and nearly as many phone calls and letters. National security advisor Condoleeza Rice, a DU alumna, sent her regards and said a picture of the team was displayed prominently on her desk. Dr. M. Dianne Murphy received two phone calls from former coach Murray Armstrong, the leader of DU's five previous national championship teams.

"That meant a lot because he has always been so gracious to me," Murphy said. "There were a lot of phone calls from our hockey alums. Hearing from people from the program, then from personal friends and colleagues who knew how much of this job I put myself into…all the messages really meant a lot to everyone involved."

The team was paraded around the city. Unlike their rivals in the Western Collegiate Hockey Association, the Pioneers have to work harder for their fan base in Denver, a city that has teams in all four of the primary professional sports leagues as well as numerous other entertainment and athletic distractions that can't be found in Grand Forks, North Dakota or Anchorage, Alaska. Denver's sports fans came together in a hurry to support the Pioneers, and they were eager to voice their congratulations once the team came home with the trophy.

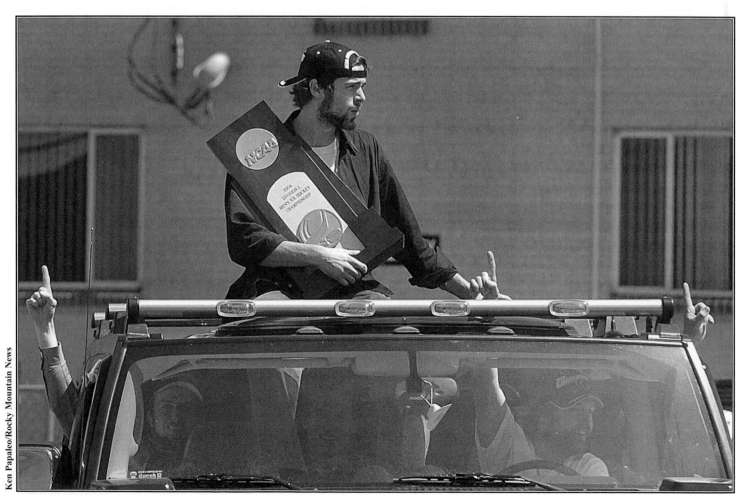

Ken Papaleo/Rocky Mountain News

Ryan Caldwell perches atop Greg Keith's monstrous Hummer with the national championship trophy for a joyride around campus after the team returned from Boston.

A rally at Magness Arena attracted over 3,000 supporters as well as a guest list that included Governor Bill Owens. The team threw out the first pitch at a Colorado Rockies game at Coors Field, with Caldwell whipping a strike to Adam Berkhoel, his final glove save in a DU jersey. The Colorado State Senate drafted an official honor for the championship team, and later that week they were recognized on the ice during an NHL playoff game between the Colorado Avalanche and the Dallas Stars. The thunderous ovation delivered by the sold-out crowd at the Pepsi Center chilled the Pioneers.

"We had some great times," Bull said. "I think the standing ovation we got at the Pepsi Center during the Avs game was the greatest moment. It really brought everything into perspective, how many fans we have in Denver and how awesome our sport is."

For months Chancellor Ritchie could not stop his eyes from welling whenever he recalled the tumult of emotions that washed over him in the final moments of the championship. Ritchie became involved with the university in 1983 and became the school's 16th Chancellor in 1989. While hockey always had been the prominent athletics program at Denver, Ritchie and Dr. M. Dianne Murphy led a movement that brought all the school's other sports to the Division I level in 1998. The campus is stocked with new athletic venues and facilities, yet DU's flagship sport had never reached the Frozen Four during Ritchie's tenure.

Getting there and finally winning the championship left him giddy with excitement, which became a constant affliction, since congratulatory messages were pouring into his office.

"I was surprised by the size of the reaction. Not only here in Denver, but around the country and even around the globe," Ritchie said. "There were people I hadn't heard from in years, or people who I didn't think knew what a hockey puck was, that watched the game. Personally, I think the quality of the game made people

Ryan Caldwell (left) and coach George Gwozdecky (right), receive an autographed stick from Colorado Avalanche player Jim Cummins. The Pioneers were given a resounding standing ovation when they were introduced to a sold-out crowd at the Pepsi Center during an Avalanche playoff game.

Tim De Frisco/De Frisco Photography

Rocky Mountain News

CHAMPION PIONEERS LOSING LOTS OF SLEEP, LOVING IT; MAGNESS ARENA RALLY BRINGS OUT VIPS AND GOALIE FROM 1968-69

Wednesday, April 14, 2004
By Pat Rooney
SPECIAL TO THE NEWS

Sleep deprivation is a way of life for most college students. Since Saturday, though, the University of Denver hockey team has been enveloped in a whirlwind that has made sleep all but impossible.

Not that any of the Pioneers are complaining.

DU continued its celebration of the team's sixth national championship on Tuesday with a rally at Magness Arena.

An estimated 3,100 fans attended the event, which featured guest speeches by Gov. Bill Owens, Chancellor Dan Ritchie and former goal-tender Gerry Powers, one of the leaders of the Pioneers' championship teams of 1968 and 1969.

"The reception we got from people around Denver is just amazing," DU captain Ryan Caldwell said. "All the media attention and all the attention the guys are getting is well-deserved. We've probably gotten about eight hours of sleep since we got back from Boston, but I don't think anyone is tired."

The Pioneers are getting accustomed to being in front of cameras and microphones, and their fan base is blossoming. Gov. Owens proudly displayed the L.L. Bean parka and boots he won in a wager with Maine Gov. John Elias Baldacci. The Pioneers will be honored at the Rockies game tonight and at the Avalanche playoff game Saturday.

"The support, even from people you don't expect, has been awesome," senior Connor James said. "Going around campus, going out to eat . . . we bring the trophy everywhere, and everyone wants to take your picture or shake your hand. It's been great to give something back not only to the University of Denver, but to the city of Denver, as well. The support has been unbelievable. I hope it keeps on going."

Perhaps the most heartfelt tribute was given by Powers. Before the ceremony, he showed the Pioneers' the 1969 championship trophy, his jersey from the two championship seasons and his old face mask, a battered relic straight out of a *Friday the 13th* movie.

Powers jokingly expressed relief that goalie Adam Berkhoel fell one short of his career record of 13 shutouts, although Berkhoel's 1-0 shutout against Maine in the final pulled him even with Powers' single-season record of seven. Powers also mentioned Keith Magnuson, a former DU standout who died in a car accident in December.

Before Tuesday's ceremony, Powers wondered if it was a helping hand from above that nudged the skate of a Maine player into the crease, forcing an early goal by the Black Bears to be disallowed.

"It's a situation we've all been waiting for," Powers said. "The only regret we have is that (Magnuson) isn't here with us to see it. There was no bigger supporter of the University of Denver. To have that happen right before Christmas, then have all this come together, there is something weird about it."

Ryan Caldwell fires a strike to goaltender Adam Berkhoel while throwing out the first pitch at a Colorado Rockies game. The Pioneers were stunned by the size and enthusiasm of the reaction of Denver sports fans to their national championship.

talk about it more. Even some of the old-timers who have seen 30 or 40 Frozen Fours said they had never seen anything like that before."

The team enjoyed its most overwhelming congratulatory appearance on May 19, 2004, when the Pioneers were honored by President George W. Bush at the White House. During the ceremony at the nation's capital, M. Dianne Murphy was struck by the type of unpredictable moment the late Keith Magnuson had prepared the team for months earlier. As President Bush greeted the team and Coach Gwozdecky, Denver's athletics director was on the periphery of the crowd, basking in the light of the players' beaming smiles. She had a sense the glow reached all the way back to Denver and even beyond.

"To see those guys, how sharp they looked and to see them smiling, and to see George smiling, that's what it's all about. To be there to see it was wonderful. That part of the journey is over. But really, we're just getting started."

The trophy accompanied the team everywhere throughout the extended chaos of their victory celebration. It suffered an inordinate amount of wear-and-tear while surviving such festive accidents as an ill-fated thrust into a twirling ceiling fan. Eventually, while some future DU team is embarking on a new journey, the hardware will grow dusty in its display case at Magness Arena. When members of the championship team return from time to time over the years, they're bound to chuckle at the nicks and scratches marring the trophy's finish. Perhaps their wives and children will give them curious glances, wondering about the stories behind the sudden bursts of laughter. Likely the guys will mumble that it's nothing, or maybe they will answer by simply showing off the matching commemorative tattoos they all got in one final act of team unity.

That's about the best explanation they will be able to supply, since it would be impossible to describe all the joy, heartache, and triumph that will return in a rush with their first glance at the trophy. And if passing fans ever question why the trophy is so dinged, why someone over the years hasn't endeavored to give it the facelift it so obviously needs, they should first understand this: Few, if any, championship trophies have ever been so appropriately scarred.

The University of Denver Pioneers of 2003-04 were as resilient as the hardware they brought home. They absorbed a tremendous amount of punishment, enough that a few players will forever bear physical scars. They were chipped and battered from every angle, yet they withstood the bombardment until they were the last team standing. They learned from their own underachieving performances at midseason. They matured from the talent and wisdom they shared with each other. And they were inspired to greatness by the lessons gleaned from the unfortunate passing of the team's most beloved hockey alum, Keith Magnuson.

Much like the shine of their trophy, the brilliance of the Pioneers' triumph was magnified by the countless hurdles they conquered throughout their magically tumultuous Journey.

"The more you think about the season, someone was looking out for us," Scott McConnell said. "I don't know if it was Maggie. I don't know who it was. Like my dad said about the final, the hockey Gods were in our favor that night. That's something that can never be taken away from us. Whoever it was, Thank You."

Sandy Hubbard

Juniors Luke Fulghum and Jon Foster, freshman Glenn Fisher and junior Jussi Halme take in the view atop a fire truck as the Pioneers serve as the grand marshals in the Cultural Day Parade in Denver on May 1, 2004.

Denver Hockey Player Bios

Adam Berkhoel (Woodbury, Minn.): The senior goaltender was at his best down the stretch, notching 1-0 shutouts in two of DU's final three games, including the championship game against Maine. Berkhoel tied for the national lead with seven shutouts, which also matched DU's single-season record set by Gerry Powers during the 1967-68 season. Berkhoel finished his career with 12 shutouts, one short of Powers' all-time record of 13, and he also ranks seventh with 55 career wins. Berkhoel is second on DU's career chart in saves percentage (.911) and he ranks fourth with a goals-against average of 2.47. Berkhoel went 24-11-4 during the championship season, stopping 104 of 109 shots during the NCAA tournament. Berkhoel was named the Most Outstanding Player of the West Regional, an honor he repeated at the Frozen Four. Berkhoel was honored by *USA Hockey* as the College Player of the Year.

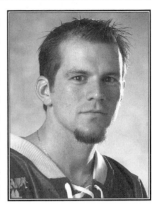

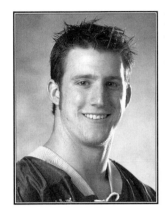

Max Bull (Faribault, Minn.): Bull, one of the team's alternate captains, was one of only three Pioneers skaters to appear in all 44 games. The senior forward finished the 2003-2004 season with two goals and 12 assists, capping his career with 16 goals and 30 assists in 154 games. Bull produced the biggest point of his career when his blistering slap shot against North Dakota in the West Regional final was redirected by Luke Fulghum, resulting in DU's only goal in its 1-0 victory and giving Bull a spot on the All-West Regional team. A rugged two-way player, Bull became the second member in his family to win a national championship, following in the footsteps of his older brother Jesse, who won the title with North Dakota in 1997. Bull provided help along the blue-line when many of DU's defensemen were sidelined at midseason.

Ryan Caldwell (Deloraine, Manitoba): The gutsy captain led the Pioneers to the championship despite chronically aching knees that kept him out of practice for most of the second half of the season. Caldwell was one of the highest-scoring defensemen in the country, posting 15 goals after scoring only 11 in 114 games coming into the season. His final goal pulled DU into a tie with Minnesota-Duluth in the third period of the national semifinals. Caldwell finished his career ranked among DU's top nine defensemen in points (88), goals (26), and assists (62). Although Caldwell shed his penchant for taking ill-timed penalties, a habit that plagued his first three seasons, Caldwell still finished fourth on DU's career penalty minutes chart with 306. Caldwell was voted the team's most inspirational player and was named the Defensive Player of the Year in the WCHA.

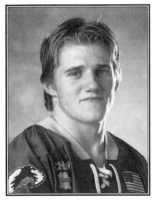

Matt Carle (Anchorage, Alaska): The freshman standout became the first American-born player to win a gold medal at the U.S. World Junior championship and capture an NCAA national championship. Carle, a steady defenseman, tallied 25 points on five goals and 20 assists despite missing 14 games because of an ankle injury and his national team duties. Carle produced a pair of four-point games and had an eight-game point streak from February 21 through March 26. Carle was the team's leading scorer during its nine-game unbeaten streak with three goals and 16 assists. He was named the WCHA Rookie of the Week three times and also earned one WCHA Defensive Player of the Week award. Carle also was named to the WCHA All-Rookie team.

Denver Hockey Player Bios

J.D. Corbin (Littleton, Colo.): The freshman wing established himself as the heir apparent to Connor James as the team's fastest skater. Corbin tallied his first career point with an assist at Alaska Anchorage on November 15, 2003, and notched his first career goal two weeks later against Findlay. He completed his rookie campaign with three goals and six assists.

Lukas Dora (Lednice, Czech Republic): Dora was the Pioneers' third-leading scorer, capping his senior season with 36 points on 14 goals and 22 assists. The feisty right wing led the Pioneers' 5-3 win against Minnesota-Duluth in the national semifinals with a goal and two assists, scoring the game-winning goal in the third period. Dora played much of the season with a wrist injury that required surgery just days after the national championship game, yet he remained one of the team's most productive players. A fixture on DU's special teams, Dora recorded six power-play goals and one shorthanded goal. Dora was named to the all-tournament team of the Wells Fargo Denver Cup after posting two assists and the game-winning goal in the championship game against Nebraska-Omaha. He finished his career with 97 points.

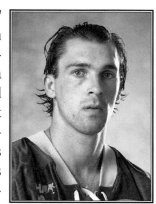

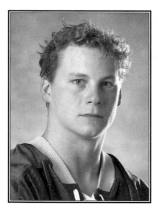

Jeff Drummond (Leduc, Alberta): Drummond began the season by earning the MVP award at the Lefty McFadden Tournament, leading the Pioneers to a pair of victories with three goals and an assist. Drummond, a junior forward, produced two points in each of the Pioneers' first three games and put together a six-game point-scoring streak from January 24 through February 20. Drummond scored a career-best 28 points in 2003-2004 on 13 goals and 15 assists.

Glenn Fisher (Edmonton, Alberta): Fisher appeared in nine games during his rookie campaign, posting a record of 3-1-1 with a saves percentage of .872 and a goals-against average of 3.58. Fisher won his first career start, making 22 saves in DU's 6-3 win against Northeastern on October 18, 2003. Fisher was named to the all-tournament team of the Wells Fargo Denver Cup after making a season-high 36 saves in the Pioneers' tournament-opening win against Niagara. Fisher also notched his first career assist against Niagara.

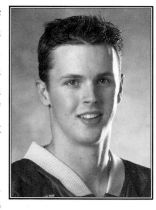

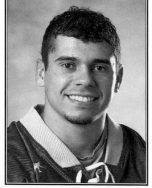

Jon Foster (Suffern, New York): The junior forward had a goal and an assist in the Pioneers' season-opening victory against Ohio State, eventually finishing the season with 12 goals and six assists. Foster was second on the team with seven power-play goals and tied for third with three game-winning goals. Foster had two points in each game of Denver's sweep of Minnesota State, Mankato at Magness Arena in mid-February.

Denver Hockey Player Bios

Luke Fulghum (Colorado Springs, Colo.): The native Coloradoan was the Pioneers' good luck charm, as the team produced an 18-0-2 record in games that saw the junior forward notch a point. In front of his hometown crowd at the West Regional final, Fulghum's tip of a Max Bull shot resulted in the only goal of DU's 1-0 win against North Dakota. Fulghum also scored the Pioneers' first goal of the Frozen Four against Minnesota-Duluth, adding a gutsy assist on Ryan Caldwell's game-tying goal in the third period. Fulghum was named to the Lefty McFadden All-Tournament team and finished the season with 14 goals and nine assists.

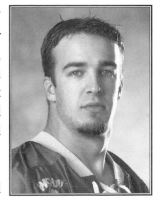

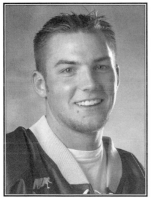

Gabe Gauthier (Buena Park, Calif.): The sophomore center had a breakout season in 2003-04, developing into one of the top scorers in the WCHA. Gauthier shook off a disappointing freshman campaign to lead the Pioneers in points (43), goals (18), game-winning goals (6) and power play goals (8). Gauthier also shared the team lead in assists with 25. Gauthier posted 10 multi-point games, and he capped his memorable season by scoring DU's only goal in the team's 1-0 victory in the national championship game against Maine. Gauthier, a third-team All-WCHA selection, helped Denver average 3.39 goals a game, the eighth-best mark in the nation.

Jussi Halme (Nokia, Finland): Halme missed six midseason games because of a broken jaw he suffered after sacrificing himself to block a shot at Minnesota State in late December, yet he returned to become one of DU's steadiest defenders down the stretch. Halme scored his only game-winning goal of the season against Northeastern on November 17, finishing the season with two goals and 11 assists. Halme, who was honored on the WCHA's All-Academic team, scored a short-handed goal against Findlay on November 28.

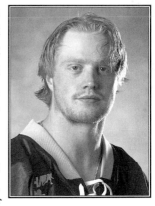

Mike Handza (Glenshaw, Penn.): Handza played in all 44 games for the Pioneers, the most appearances by any of DU's freshmen. Handza notched his first career point on an assist in the finale of the Northeastern series in October. He scored his first career goal at Michigan Tech on February 21, 2004, and he earned assists in back-to-back games against Colorado College in March. Handza finished the season with a goal and four assists.

Ryan Helgason (Woodbury, Minn.): Helgason, a freshman forward, played in 32 games, recording three goals and two assists. Helgason scored his first career goal at Minnesota State, Mankato on December 19, 2003, and scored goals in each game of the Wells Fargo Denver Cup a week later. He notched his first career point with an assist on J.D. Corbin's first career goal against Findlay.

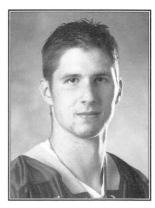

Denver Hockey Player Bios

Connor James (Calgary, Alberta): The senior left wing displayed grit in the NCAA tournament reminiscent of former NBA great Willis Reed, shrugging off a broken right fibula that had not completely healed to record a goal and two assists at the Frozen Four. James was DU's second-leading scorer, compiling 13 goals and a team-leading 25 assists in 40 games. James finished his career tied for 18th on the Pioneers' career scoring list with 150 points. James also is tied for 15th in career assists with 93. James earned the MVP award of the Wells Fargo Denver Cup with three assists in two games. The final assist of his career came on the winning play of the national championship game against Maine, as Gabe Gauthier converted a pinpoint centering pass from James for DU's only goal. A finance/marketing major, James was named the WCHA's Student Athlete of the Year.

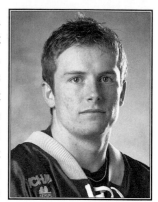

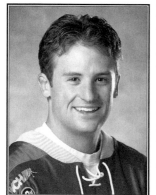

Jon James (Arnold, Md.): James did not appear in a game during the regular season, yet the freshman defenseman gave the Pioneers much-needed practice help when many of the team's blueliners were sidelined at midseason. James played in DU's exhibition games against the U.S. Under-18 National team and the University of British Columbia.

Greg Keith (Delta, British Columbia): A fiery senior forward, the versatile Keith finished his career ranked seventh on DU's career penalty minutes list with 279. Keith had 10 goals and eight assists during his senior campaign, finishing his career with 30 goals and 27 assists. Keith had an assist and an empty-net goal during the Pioneers' 5-3 win against Minnesota-Duluth in the national semifinals. One of the team's emotional leaders, Keith led the Pioneers with 97 penalty minutes, the ninth-highest single-season mark in team history.

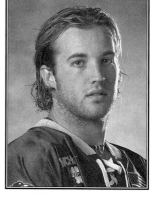

Danny King (Colorado Springs, Colo.): As the team's third goaltender, King didn't crack the lineup while toiling behind Adam Berkhoel and fellow rookie Glenn Fisher. But King was a valuable practice player, particularly when Fisher was sidelined with nagging injuries in December.

Matt Laatsch (Lakeville, Minn.): The burly 6-foot-3 defenseman rebounded from an injury-plagued sophomore season to become one of the Pioneers' most durable players, appearing in 41 of 44 games. Laatsch scored his first career goal at Minnesota State on December 20, one night after posting only the second two-point game of his career. He gave DU a 2-0 lead in the team's NCAA first-round game against Miami of Ohio with a scorching wrist shot from deep along the left wing, earning a spot on the All-West Regional team. Laatsch, who had five goals and seven assists, will be the Pioneers' captain in 2004-2005.

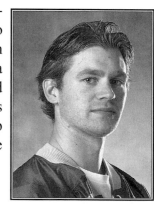

Denver Hockey Player Bios

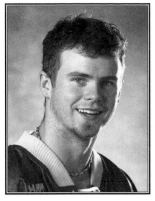

Nick Larson (Moorhead, Minn.): The most blue-collar performer among the Pioneers' blueliners, the junior persevered to become a regular among DU's defensive corps down the stretch. Larson battled through nagging knee and ankle problems to play in 30 games, including the final 15 in a row. Larson produced his first career point with an assist during DU's 3-0 win at Michigan Tech on February 21, 2004. Larson, who was voted the team's most improved player, also scored a goal during an exhibition game against the University of British Columbia.

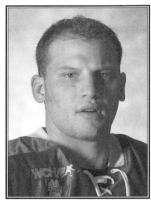

Scott McConnell (Colorado Springs, Colo.): The witty, jovial native Coloradoan played in only one game, yet his unflappable personality made McConnell as important a leader as any of DU's seniors. McConnell played in five games as a junior and one as a senior, suiting up for the Minnesota-Duluth game at home on January 9, 2004. McConnell became the fourth person in his family to win a national championship, following in the footsteps of his uncles, Mark and Pete Johnson, and his grandfather Bob Johnson, all of whom won titles at Wisconsin.

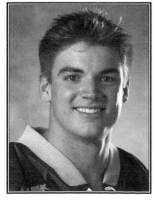

Brock McMorris (Cherry Hills, Colo.): A redshirt freshman from suburban Denver, McMorris appeared in six early-season games for the Pioneers, providing depth at midseason when injuries decimated DU's lineup. McMorris dressed for demanding WCHA road games at Air Force, St. Cloud State, and Minnesota State, Mankato.

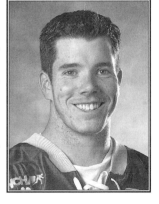

Ted O'Leary (Arvada, Colo.): Another native Coloradoan, O'Leary played a huge role in DU's lineup down the stretch, filling in admirably for Connor James when the senior suffered a broken leg in the regular season finale and replacing the suspended Lukas Dora in the national championship game. O'Leary notched a goal and four assists in 19 games, recording his first career multi-point game with two assists against Nebraska-Omaha in the championship game of the Wells Fargo Denver Cup. O'Leary scored his first career goal against Colorado College in the first game of the WCHA playoffs. O'Leary, who finished his sophomore year with a 3.95 grade point average as a biology major, earned the Dr. Art Mason Award as the team's top scholar-athlete.

Jeff Rogers (Colorado Springs, Colo.): The freshman forward played in three games for the Pioneers, taking shifts against Alaska Anchorage on November 15, 2003; Findlay on November 28; and Air Force on November 29. Like many of DU's younger players, Rogers provided a huge lift in practice when injuries struck the Pioneers' stars.

Chancellor Daniel L. Ritchie

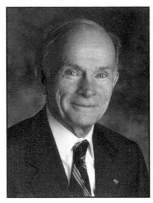

Chancellor Daniel L. Ritchie: Few people at the University of Denver were as emotionally touched by the Pioneers' national championship as Ritchie, who, in 1989, became the school's 16th Chancellor and greatest champion. Ritchie's involvement with DU began in 1983 when he joined the school's board of trustees. As Chancellor, Ritchie has spearheaded the revitalization of DU that has included a capital campaign that raised $274 million, construction of 11 new buildings with more on the way, raising academic standards and transition of the Pioneers' intercollegiate athletics programs to Division I. Reflecting the importance that Ritchie places on athletics and overall wellness as a key component of higher education, the Pioneers' home ice is in the Daniel L. Ritchie Center for Sports & Wellness, opened in 1999. His prominence in the Denver civic and cultural community and commitment to philanthropic and volunteer organizations has resulted in countless awards and boosted the University's stature in the community. Ritchie holds an AB (1954) and an MBA (1956) from Harvard University and honorary doctorate degrees from Regis University (Doctor of Education, 1992) and Catawba College (Doctor of Humane Letters, 1998).

Director of Athletics and Recreation
Dr. M. Dianne Murphy

Director of Athletics and Recreation Dr. M. Dianne Murphy: Murphy attended Tennessee Technological University in Cookeville, Tennessee, where she earned a B.S. degree in Health and Physical Education in 1972 and a M.A. degree in 1973. She earned her Ph.D. in administration, supervision and curriculum at The Florida State University in 1980. Professional work experience consists of coaching volleyball and basketball at Shorter College in Rome, Georgia. Additional professional work experience includes serving as head women's basketball coach at Florida State University and Eastern Kentucky University. She also served as Assistant Athletics Director and Chairperson of the Division of Health, Physical Education and Recreation at Kentucky State University. Dr. Murphy was the Assistant Athletics Director for External Operations at The University of Iowa from 1988-1995, and the Associate Athletics Director and Senior  Woman Administrator at Cornell University from 1995-1998. Currently she is the Director of Athletics and Recreation at the University of Denver. Murphy was named the Athletic Director of the Year for the West Region by the National Association of Collegiate Directors of Athletics for 2003-2004. She was also named the Women's Basketball Coaches Association Administrator of the Year in 2004.

Denver Hockey Assistant Coaches

Steve Miller: "Killer," as he is known among the Pioneers, has spent 10 seasons at Denver and 13 as an assistant to head coach George Gwozdecky. A graduate of St. Mary's (Minn.) University, Miller began his coaching career as an assistant at his alma mater in 1988. Miller joined Gwozdecky's staff at Miami of Ohio in 1991 and followed Gwozdecky to Denver in 1994. As Gwozdecky's top assistant, Miller has served as Denver's recruiting coordinator since 1996. Miller has recruited or coached such NHL players as Antti Laaksonen, Mark Rycroft, Matt Pettinger and Wade Dubielewicz. He has coached 22 All-WCHA honorees at the University of Denver. Miller and his wife, Heidi, have three children - Alexis, Cole, and Connor.

Seth Appert: Appert came to Denver in 1997 as a volunteer assistant coach and was promoted to a full-time assistant prior to the 1999-2000 season. He is one of the primary recruiters for DU's program, and his on-ice work with the Pioneers' goaltenders helped the development of the best goaltending tandem in the nation with Wade Dubielewicz and Adam Berkhoel for two seasons. Appert has recruited or coached three All-Americans, 16 All-WCHA selections and one Frozen Four Most Outstanding Player. He began his coaching career at his alma mater, Ferris State, as a student assistant during the 1996-97 season. He was a four-year letterwinner at Ferris State as a goaltender. Appert received a master's degree in sports management at the University of Denver in 1999. Appert and his wife Jill reside in Denver.

David Tenzer: DU's Director of Hockey Operations followed his instincts by leaving a successful law career to become the Pioneers' volunteer assistant coach in 2001. Tenzer began his coaching career in youth hockey, guiding teams in the Boulder Valley Hockey Association from 1991 through 1998. He also coached the club team at Colorado State University from 1998 through 2001. Tenzer earned a bachelor's degree in journalism at New York University in 1984 and earned his law degree at NYU in 1988. Tenzer was admitted to the Colorado Bar in 1991 and worked in Boulder from 1991 through 1995. Tenzer and his wife, Ana, live in Boulder with their son Adam.

Chris LaPerle: Denver's volunteer assistant coach in 2003-04. LaPerle spent two seasons as an assistant at Southern New Hampshire University before coming to Denver, helping to guide SNHU to a pair of Eastern College Athletic Conference Division II tournament berths. LaPerle was a four-year letterwinner from 1997-2001 at New Hampshire College. The New Hampshire native earned a bachelor's degree in education in 2001 at NHC and a master's degree in sport administration at SNHU in 2003. At Denver, LaPerle helped break down game films and aided in individual skill development at practice.

Denver Hockey Support Staff

Heather Weems: The national championship season capped Weems' first year as the University of Denver's Associate Athletics Director for Internal Operations. Primarily, Weems serves as the academic counselor for the hockey and gymnastics teams. Under Weems' guidance the Pioneers placed eight players on the WCHA's All-Academic team, and senior Connor James was named the WCHA's student-athlete of the year. Before taking her current job, Weems spent two years as Denver's Associate Athletics Director for Student-Athlete Support Services. She graduated from the University of Iowa with a B.S. in psychology and earned a master's degree in higher education from the University of Denver in 1999.

Erik Rasmussen: Rasmussen completed his seventh season at DU, his fifth as the school's Director of Sports Medicine. Rasmussen had his hands full with the rash of Pioneer injuries at midseason, and his dedication was a big reason why senior Connor James was able to make a swift return from a broken fibula to play in the Frozen Four. Rasmussen served as a student assistant at the University of Iowa for three years before moving to Denver.

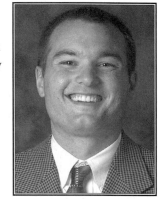

Lee Greseth: A college hockey veteran, Greseth completed his fourth season as the Pioneers' equipment manager. Greseth was the equipment manager for three years at WCHA rival North Dakota, where he enjoyed a national championship in 2000. Greseth also has worked at Alaska Anchorage, Colorado College and Minnesota.

Mike Sanders: Sanders has served four years at the University of Denver, the past two as the Pioneers' head strength and conditioning coach. Sanders oversees all 17 of Denver's varsity programs. He graduated from Nebraska-Kearney with a Bachelor of Arts in Health and Physical Education in 1996 and earned Master of Arts in Education at the University of Nebraska in 1999. Sanders spent three seasons as the assistant strength and conditioning coach at Nebraska-Kearney before taking the same job at DU in 2000.

Erich Bacher: Bacher was the primary media contact for the Pioneers' national championship season, serving as a liaison for the print, radio and television media's coverage of the hockey team. Bacher has spent two seasons at DU after working two years as a Venue Press Services Supervisor at the 2002 Olympic Winter Games in Salt Lake City, Utah. Bacher coordinated the services of over 3,000 print and photo media members at five ice venues. He will work as a press officer for the National Hockey League at the 2004 World Cup of Hockey in Helsinki, Finland and Cologne, Germany.

Part V -
A Look Back at
DU Glory

Hints of greatness? A foreshadowing of the legendary players that soon would pass through the campus?

Not at all. In fact, those were the last thoughts on the minds of anyone who witnessed the University of Denver play its first hockey game on December 19, 1949. Within a decade DU would begin to establish itself as the premier hockey institution in the country. Five national championships were won between 1958 and 1969. Players would pass through DU Arena destined for greatness in the National Hockey League. Denver quickly became a distant cry from the team that suffered through a nightmare debut in 1949.

Under the leadership of coach Vern Turner, the Pioneers could only watch as Saskatchewan scored a touchdown in each of the first two periods before adding a field goal in the third in a 17-0 trouncing of DU in the program's first game.

After losing their first nine games, the Pioneers finally earned their first victory over five weeks later with an 8-7 decision against Wyoming, but much of DU's inaugural season played out like the first game. Denver lost games by scores of 16-0, 10-0, 14-1, 18-3, and 23-2. They finished 4-13 and lost all four games to in-state rival Colorado College.

Turner began the program's turnaround the following year, guiding DU to an 11-11-1 mark before retiring with a two-year record of 15-24-1.

The first coach in DU hockey history, Vern Turner was behind the bench when the Pioneers played their first game on December 19, 1949. Turner compiled a 15-24-1 (.367) record in two seasons at DU.

Neil Celley took over as DU's second coach prior to the 1951-52 season. An NCAA tournament hero just a few months earlier for the University of Michigan, Celley became DU's coach at the age of 24. In February of 1951 Celley posted a hat trick to lead a Michigan sweep over the Pioneers. That fall Celley led DU to an upset win on his alma mater's home ice.

Celley led DU to an 18-6 record in his first season. His five-year tenure produced a record of 81-43-6, and he is responsible for putting Pioneers hockey on the map. Then Murray Armstrong came in and made sure Denver was illustrated with a huge, triumphant star on the hockey map.

A former NHL player with Toronto, Detroit, and the New York Americans, Armstrong arrived before the 1956-57 season and led the program to its 100th victory that year. The following season, Denver collected its first national championship with a 6-2 win against North Dakota in Minneapolis.

Neil Celley helped put Pioneers hockey on the map, compiling a record of 81-43-6 in five seasons. Celley was a member of the 1948 U.S. Olympic team.

The Pioneers won another national championship two years later, defeating Michigan Tech 5-3 to capture the 1960 championship trophy. Yet what had become most impressive about Armstrong's team was how they fared against elite international competition. That year saw the Pioneers skate to a win and a tie against the United States Olympic team. They defeated the Olympic teams from Sweden and West Germany and also claimed a 2-2 draw against the Russian National team.

Armstrong, nicknamed "The Chief," had won two national championships and averaged over 21 wins during his first four seasons. But his fifth team, DU's squad of 1960-61, is still regarded as one of the best college hockey teams ever assembled. Five of those players, as well as Armstrong, already are inducted as individuals into the DU Athletics Hall of Fame. The rest of the team will join them when the squad is inducted en masse in the fall of 2004.

The Pioneers of '60-61 amassed a record of 30-1-1 and finished the season with 17 consecutive wins. Denver rolled to a 12-2 victory in the NCAA title game against St. Lawrence, producing an NCAA tournament single-game record 30 points (12 goals, 18 assists). Captain Bill Masterton led the way

The 1957-58 Pioneers captured the school's first NCAA national championship with a 6-2 win over North Dakota.

with three goals and two assists. The '60-61 team still holds the DU records for points per game (17.44), goals per game (7.56), assists per game (9.88), and goals-against average (1.84). Jerry Walker set a school record that still stands with 56 goals and 10 hat tricks in the '60-61 season. The *Hockey News* named DU's '60-61 squad the best team ever as part of its 50th anniversary celebration.

In five seasons Murray had collected three NCAA championships, but he hardly was done. Denver lost the championship game in 1963 and 1964 but returned to glory in 1968 behind a cast of players led by goaltender Gerry Powers, defenseman Keith Magnuson, and forwards Jim Wiste, Craig Patrick, Tom Miller, and Robert Trembecky.

Denver's Bill Masterton was selected to the NCAA 50th Anniversary team in 1997. Masterton helped lead the Pioneers to consecutive NCAA titles in 1960-61.

DU captured the 1968 national championship with a 4-0 victory against North Dakota in the final. Trembecky scored two of DU's four third-period goals and Powers made 22 saves to pitch the first shutout ever in the championship game. There would be only one other title-game shutout in the next 35 years before DU's Adam Berkhoel accomplished the feat in 2004.

Murray Armstrong made the DU program legendary, leading the Pioneers to 11 Frozen Four appearances and five national championships. Armstrong went 460-215-31 (.674) in 21 seasons.

DU completed its second back-to-back championship the following year with a 4-3 victory against Cornell in the title match. Tied 2-2 going into the third, Trembecky and Miller scored goals to give the Pioneers their fifth national championship.

Armstrong continued to coach through the 1976-77 season, leading the Pioneers to the title game once again in 1973. Armstrong completed his 21-year career with a mark of 460-215-31 and an overflowing trophy case. In 1961 he was named the winner of the Spencer Penrose Award as the National Coach of the Year, and he earned two Coach of the Year honors in the WCHA ('61 and '68). Armstrong led the Pioneers to 11 Frozen Four appearances and eight WCHA championships. His 14 wins in the Frozen Four still rank second all-time, and only Vic Heyliger, who led Michigan to six titles between 1948 and 1956, has more national championships than Armstrong.

Marshall Johnston, the captain

The 1968-69 Pioneers, led by Keith Magnuson, won the school's fifth NCAA national championship with a 4-3 win over Cornell at Broadmoor Arena in Colorado Springs, Colo.

of DU's national runner-up team in 1963, replaced his mentor and led DU to the WCHA regular season championship in his first season, finishing 33-6-1 and earning the WCHA Coach of the Year award. That mark was the second-best winning percentage in school history, but the Pioneers were denied a chance to play for the Frozen Four because of an NCAA probation.

A former DU captain, Marshall Johnston earned WCHA Coach of the Year honors in 1977-78 after leading DU to the league title with a record of 33-6-1.

Johnston compiled a record of 89-63-7 before leaving DU after four seasons to join the New Jersey Devils as an assistant coach. Ralph Backstrom took over before the 1981-82 season, leading DU to a 21-19-3 record in his first season. Backstrom led the Pioneers back to the Frozen Four in 1986 with one of the highest-scoring teams in school history.

DU amassed a program-best 646 points that season and received some of the best single-season performances in team history. Dallas Gaume, DU's all-time leading scorer with 266 points, set single-season scoring records with 67 assists and 99 points. In any other season, Dwight Mathiasen's 89 points would have established the new school mark.

The Pioneers of '86 fell in the Frozen Four semifinals against

Ralph Backstrom led DU to its first Frozen Four appearance in 13 years in 1986 with the highest-scoring team in Pioneers history. Backstrom coached Denver to 182 wins in nine seasons.

Harvard and lost to Minnesota in the now-defunct third-place game. It would be Denver's last appearance on the national stage for a long, long time.

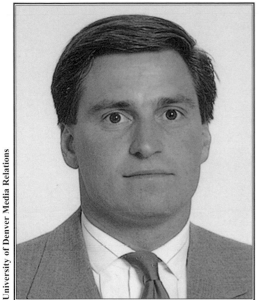

Frank Serratore was only 49-92-9 (.357) in four seasons, but he helped implement many of the upgrades of the Pioneers' facilities.

Backstrom left DU on the heels of an 18-24 season in 1989-90, completing his nine-year tenure with a record of 182-174-14. The failure in 1986 began a tailspin that would hinder the program for years.

Frank Serratore followed Backstrom and suffered through a 6-30-2 season, the lowest win total since DU's inaugural 1949-50 season. The team went 9-25-2 the next year, marking the first time DU had three consecutive losing seasons.

By the time George Gwozdecky arrived from Miami (Ohio) before the 1994-95 season, DU had become a footnote in the WCHA and invisible on the national scene. Gwozdecky began to turn things around immediately, leading his first team to a 25-15-2 mark and the Pioneers' first berth in the NCAA tournament since '86. DU returned to the NCAA tournament in 1997 and 1999, with the '99 squad winning the WCHA playoffs for the first time since 1986.

Gwozdecky led a historical season in 2001-02. The Pioneers earned their first No. 1 ranking in the national polls. They became the first team in 11 years to win the MacNaughton Cup as the WCHA's regular season champ as well as the league tournament. DU went 32-8-1, winning a school-record nine games in a row to start the season. Goalie Wade Dubielewicz earned second-team All-American honors after setting single-season DU records for saves percentage (.943) and goals against average (1.72).

George Gwozdecky is only the second coach to win 200 games at DU. The Pioneers' title in 2004 made Gwozdecky the first person to win a national championship as a player, assistant coach, and head coach.

Gwozdecky earned the WCHA Coach of the Year award and finished second in the race for the Spencer Penrose Award, which was given to Maine's Tim Whitehead. Gwozdecky didn't mind letting Whitehead have that trophy, since the Pioneers collected the national championship trophy with a 1-0 win against Whitehead's Black Bears in 2004. That victory left Gwozdecky with a career record of 223-152-31 record in 10 seasons at DU.

In 55 seasons of hockey, the University of Denver has won six national championships, 11 WCHA regular-season championships, and a league-leading 13 WCHA tournament championships. The Pioneers have produced four WCHA MVPs, two WCHA Defensive Players of the year, and seven WCHA Rookies of the Year. Following DU's 2004 national championship season, the program boasts an all-time record of 1099-763-99.

Wade Dubielewicz was named second-team All-America after he helped the Pioneers to an impressive 32-8-1 overall record in 2001-02.

Denver Hockey Timeline

1949
- Completion of DU Arena.
- Vern Turner named first coach.
- Dec. 19, 1949 - Played first game, lost to Saskatchewan 17-0.

1950
- Jan. 27, 1950 - Defeated Wyoming 8-7 for first victory.
- Feb. 18, 1950 - Defeated Wyoming 10-6 for first victory in the DU Arena.

1951
- Neil Celley named Denver's second coach
1952.
- Eddie Miller received Denver's first All-America hockey honor.

1954
- Jan. 5, 1954 - Played 100th game, defeating Michigan Tech 7-1.

1956
- Murray Armstrong begins legacy as DU hockey coach.
- Dec. 19 - Defeated Michigan State 3-1 for 100th victory.

1958
- March 7 - Denver shares its first league title (WIHL).
- March 15 - Denver wins NCAA title by defeating UND 6-2.

1959
- WCHA founded.
- Jan. 10 - Tied Russian National Team 4-4
1960.
- Feb. 5-6 - Played U.S. Olympic Team; Pioneers win 7-5 and skate to a 5-5 overtime tie.

- Feb. 8 -Tied Russian Olympic Team 2-2 in overtime.
- Feb. 13 - Defeated West German Olympic Team 5-3.
- Feb. 19 - Defeated Swedish Olympic Team 5-3.
- March 12 - WCHA playoff champions by defeating Colorado College 3-1.
- March 20 - Claimed second NCAA crown, defeating Michigan Tech 5-3.

1961
- Feb. 4 - Defeated Colorado College 7-5 for 200th victory.
- March 11 - Captured WCHA playoff championship title by defeating Michigan Tech 8-2.
- March 18 -Won NCAA crown by defeating St. Lawrence 12-2.
- Coach Armstrong receives Spencer Penrose Award as NCAA Division I Coach of the Year and WCHA Coach of the Year.

1963
- March 8 - Captured WCHA playoff titlc against North Dakota 5-4 in overtime.
- March 16 - Placed second at NCAA Tournament, losing 6-5 to North Dakota.
- March 13 - Defeated Michigan 6-2 for WCHA playoff championship and MacNaughton Cup.
- March 21 - Placed second in NCAA Tournament, losing to Michigan Tech 6-3.

1966
- Feb. 4 - Defeated Colorado College 4-1 for 300th victory.
- March 5 - Defeated North Dakota 5-4 in overtime to capture

WCHA playoff champion title.
- March 19 - Placed third at NCAA Tournament by defeating Boston University 4-3.

1967
- Jan. 28, 1967 - Played 500th game, defeated Boston University 3-1.
- Dec. 26-30, 1967 - Participated in Broadmoor World Tournament at Colorado Springs.
Dec. 26 - Tied Finnish Olympic Team 2-2.
Dec. 28 - Lost to U.S. Olympic Team 5-4.
Dec. 29 - Beat Italian Olympic Team 5-2.
Dec. 30 - Lost to Russian Olympic Team 8-1.

1968
- March 9 - Defeated Minnesota 7-3 to capture WCHA playoff title.
- March 16 - Defeated North Dakota 4-0 to win fourth NCAA title.
- Armstrong named WCHA Coach of the Year.
- Dec. 27-29 - Participated in Broadmoor World Tournament.
Dec. 27 - Beat U.S. National Team 6-0
Dec. 29 - Played Czech National Team, 2-2, game called in Denver's favor.

1969
- March 8 - Defeated Colorado College 3-1 to claim WCHA playoff championship.
- March 15 - Defeated Cornell 4-3 to win its fifth NCAA title, marking the second time back-to-back titles were won.

Denver Hockey Timeline

1970
• Feb. 20 - Defeated Michigan Tech 5-3 for 400th victory.

1971
• March 12 - Defeated Minnesota-Duluth 9-3 for WCHA playoff championship.
• March 20 - Placed third at NCAA Tournament.

1972
• March 11 - Defeated Michigan State 9-3 to win WCHA playoff title.
• March 18 - Placed fourth at NCAA Tourney

1973
• March 11 - Blanked Michigan Tech 4-0 to win WCHA playoff title.
• March 17 - Placed second at NCAA Tournament.

1974
• Feb. 1 - Defeated Minnesota 6-5 for 500th victory.

1977
• Marshall Johnston assumes coaching duties
• Pioneers win MacNaughton Cup; Johnston named WCHA Coach of the Year.

1978
• Dec. 28 - Defeated Colorado College 5-2 for 600th victory.

1980
• Nov. 1 - Played 1,000th game, defeated Northern Michigan 4-3.

1981
• Ralph Backstrom begins nine-year coaching career.

1984
• Nov. 23 - Defeated Illinois-Chicago 8-4 for 700th victory.

1986
• March 14-15 - Defeated Minnesota 3-0 and 3-2 to capture WCHA playoff title.
• March 29 - Lost to Minnesota 6-4 to place fourth at NCAA Tournament.
• Backstrom named WCHA Coach of the Year and wins Spencer Penrose Award as NCAA Division I Hockey Coach of the Year.

1989
• Jan. 20 - Defeated St. Cloud State 8-3 for 800th victory.
• Dec. 5 - Former DU player and Director of Athletics Craig Patrick named general manager of the Pittsburgh Penguins.

1990
• May 24 - Frank Serratore named head coach.
• Aug. 3, 1990 - Life-size statue of Murray Armstrong unveiled.

1991
• Feb. 16 - Rick Berens becomes the school's all-time leading goal scorer when he nets his second goal of the night before a sellout crowd vs. Colorado College at DU Arena.
• Feb. 18 - Keith Magnuson inducted into Colorado Sports Hall of Fame.

1992
• Dec. 30, 1992 - Pioneers capture first Denver Cup, defeating Notre Dame 6-1.

1993
• Jan. 15 - Played 1,500th game, lost to Minnesota-Duluth 7-1.
• Swept season series with North Dakota for the first time since the 1960-61 season.
• Dec. 29 - Won second Denver Cup title, defeated Boston College 4-2.

1994
• May 19 - George Gwozdecky named the seventh coach in Pioneer history.
• Dec. 29 - Defeat Brown 3-2, to win third Denver Cup.
• Pioneers put together a 10-game winning streak from Nov. 18 to Dec. 28.

1995
• March 4 - Won Gold Pan Trophy by winning season series against Colorado College 2-1-1.
• March 11 - Defeated Michigan Tech 5-2 for 900th victory.
• March 17 - Gwozdecky named WCHA Coach of the Year.
• March 24 - Won NCAA Tournament game against New Hampshire 9-2.
• Dec. 28 - DU defeats then-first-ranked Colorado College 3-2 before the largest crowd ever to witness a college hockey game in Colorado - 16,061 at McNichols Arena - to win its fourth straight Denver Cup title.

Denver Hockey All-Time Letterwinners

- A -

Player	Year(s)
Abbott, W. G., W-D (14, 21, 11)***	1952-55
Adams, Erik, D (4)****	1999-2002
Affleck, Bruce, D (4)***	1972-74
Aikens, Mike, D (26)*	1991
Allen, Tom, G (28, 29)**	1985-86
Alley, Tom, F (18)*	1975
Anderson, David, W (21)****	1982-85
Anderson, Glenn, W (7)*	1979
Anderson, Jim, F (11)**	1975-76
Anderson, Rob, C-W (8)****	1977-80
Andersson, Erik, C-W (26)****	1994-97
Art, Jon R., F-D (13, 2)***	1961-63
Arthur, Bradford, W (14)*	1950
Ash, Jeff (6)*	1991
Aufderheide, Walt, G (26)**	1977-78

- B -

Player	Year(s)
Badowsky, Peter, D (23, 6)**	1965-66
Bales, Jim, G (24)***	1976-78
Bannister, Lyn*	1963
Barber, Greg, F (11)****	2000-03
Barnhill, J. Allison, D (18)***	1958-60
Baron, Paul, G (29, 1)****	1988-91
Beatty, J. Trent, W (13, 16)***	1960-62
Beauchamp, Larry, G (1)**	1962-63
Beers, Ed, W (9)****	1979-82
Begg, William, G (1)**	1952,54
Belcourt, Alex, C (12)****	1976-79
Berens, Rick, W (7)****	1988-91
Berezowsky, Craig, W (17)*	1978
Berkhoel, Adam, G (24)****	2001-04
Berry, Dave, W (14)***	1981-83
Berry, Doug, C (7)**	1976-78
Berry, Ken, W (22)**	1979,81
Beutel, Rolf, W (23)**	1989-90
Bianchin, Jordan, F (9)**	2000-2001
Biggs, Darren, W (5)****	1989-92
Birenbaum, Stuart, G (1)*	1979
Bjork, Anders, C (18)****	1995-98
Blanche, Rich, W (20, 11)***	1968-70
Blom, Buddy, G (1)***	1964-66
Boake, Kingdon B., D (13)*	1967
Bohonus, Gary, W (15)*	1974
Bolin, Peter, D (3)*	1983
Bowman, Sean, D (4)*	1996
Bradley, W. Lyle, C (15)**	1965-66

Player	Year(s)
Bragnalo, Rick, C-W (11)****	1971-74
Brandt, Mitch, D (7)****	1972-75
Brooks, Dan, D (6)****	1987-90
Brown, James R., C (19)**	1958-59
Browne, Mike, D (14)*	1985
Bull, Max, F (14)****	2001-04
Burgess, Donald R., D (2, 3)***	1951-53
Burns, Chris, G (31)**	1993-94
Busniuk, Mike, D-C (5)****	1971-74
Buzan, Garrett, W (11)****	1994-97

- C -

Player	Year(s)
Caldwell, Ryan, D (21)****	2001-04
Cameron, Donald B., W (12)***	1965-67
Campbell, Chad, F (17)***	1974-76
Carefoot, Brad, F (10)***	1973-75
Carignan, Lucien, G (30)****	1988-91
Carle, Matt, D (12)*	2004-present
Carlson, Corey, W (24)****	1990-92, 94
Carruthers, Robert, W*	1953
Cary, Brent, W (15)****	1992, 94-96
Casey, Joe, F (7)**	1998,00
Chow, Wah Morse (Joe), W (22)***	1950-52
Christie, Mike, D (4)***	1970-72
Clayton, John, D (6, 21)***	1970, 72-73
Cohen, Rick, G (24)*	1979
Collie, Conrad S., W (10)***	1958-60
Comrie, Paul, F (20)****	1996-99
Congrave, George*	1958
Corbett, Mike, D (21)***	1994, 96-97
Corbin, J.D., F (11)*	2004-present
Cook, Jesse, D (20)****	1999-2002
Court, William (Dave), W (16)*	1951
Cresswell, Gordon E., W (15)**	1957-58
Cristofoli, Ed, W (18)****	1986-89

- D -

Player	Year(s)
Dairon, Mike, W (19)****	1995-98
Dalrymple, Jim, G (29)**	1983-84
Daly, Frank, G (1)**	1968-69
Davidson, Mark, W (14)****	1977-80
Davis, Calvin, C (8)*	1950
DeCorby, Ian, D (28)****	1991-94
DeLange, George, G (11)*	1950
Del Bosco, Armando, D**	1956-57
Deyarmond, Greg, C (8)*	1982
Dickson, Robert B., C (7)***	1954-56

Player	Year(s)
DiNapoli, Paul, G (20, 19)**	1960-61
Dineen, Kevin, D (9)**	1982-83
Dineen, Shawn, D (16)****	1978-81
Dingwall, W. Walter, W (7)***	1957-59
Dion, Grant, D (6)****	1983-86
Doell, Kevin, F (22)****	2000-03
Donofrio, Tony, F (6)****	1951-54
Dora, Lukas, F (13)****	2001-04
Dowhan, William R., W (13)**	1962-63
Drew, Lyle, D (21)*	1950-51
Drewicki, Scott, D (5)*	2003
Drummond, Jeff, F, (39)***	2002-present
Dubielewicz, Wade, G (31)****	2000-03
Duffus, F. Gerald, W (14)**	1961-62

- E -

Player	Year(s)
Eagle, James R., D (4)**	1965-66
Eaves, Cecil, D (5)*	1957
Ecklebarger, Kermit, W (23)***	1984-86
Elders, Jason, W (22)****	1992-95
Engevik, Glen, W (22)***	1987-89
Engstrom, Bjorn, F (17)****	1998-01

- F -

Player	Year(s)
Fairman, Jason, C (15)*	1988
Falcone, Mark, F (13)****	1975-78
Fisher, Glenn, G (28)*	2004
Fishman, Howard, G (30)*	1983
Foster, Jon, F (15)****	2002-present
Follett, Mike, C-W (19)**	1979-80
Fragomeni, Dominic, LW (15)***	1962-64
Fraser, Don, C (6)***	1980-82
Fulghum, Luke, F (17)***	2002-present

- G -

Player	Year(s)
Gagnon, John, G (1)*	1980
Gaume, Dallas, C (12)****	1983-86
Gauthier, Gabe, F (9)**	2003-present
Geddes, Louis D., W (9)***	1965-67
Geisthardt, Max R., LW (15)***	1959-61
Genovy, Allan, C-W (9)***	1968-70
Gibson, Doug, W (16)***	1971-73
Gibson, Gordon, D (6)***	1976-78
Gillard, Myles V., C-W (10)**	1964-65
Gillies, Chris, G (1)****	1986-89
Gilmore, Tom, W (12)***	1968-70

Denver Hockey All-Time Letterwinners

Player	Year(s)
Glanville, Ernie, G (1)****	1975-78
Godfrey, John S., D (8)***	1957-59
Godfrey, Peter, F-D (17, 8)**	1983-84
Gould, Timothy, D (3)***	1967-69
Gourlie, David, D (10)****	1985-88
Grahame, Ron, G (1)****	1970-73
Grahame, Jason, D (3)**	2002-03
Graiziger, Robert , C-F (19)****	1973-76
Griebel, Don*	1954
Gunther, Petri, C (8, 28)****	1994-97

- H -

Player	Year(s)
Hacker, Ryan, D (6)****	1996-99
Hall, Keith, G (1, 24)**	1970, 72
Hall, Joe, C (15)*	1979
Hall, Maurice, C (7)*	1993
Halme, Jussi, D (12, 20)**	2003-present
Hamill, Robert P., C-W (18)***	1962-64
Hamilton, Ed, D (5)***	1968-70
Hamlin, Thomas (Ray), D (3)**	1959-60
Handza, Mike, F (6)*	2004-present
Hansen, Deane, F-D (18)****	1981-84
Hanson, Sam, D (23)***	1951-53
Hanson, David, F (11, 9)****	1985-88
Hartmann, J.J., F (26, 7)****	2000-03
Hau, Jim, C (9)*	1989
Hays, Ed, C (17)****	1970-73
Helgason, Ryan, F (10)*	2004-present
Helm, Dan, D (7)**	1970-71
Henning, Marvin M., W (13)**	1964-65
Henrich, Ben, G (35)**	1998-99
Herrebout, Andrew (Ray), C (17)**	1964-65
Hill, Andy, C (11, 12)****	1979-82
Hill, Bruce, W (27)****	1985-88
Hilliard, Andy, W (25)****	1980-83
Hogan, Paul, F (16)*	1976
Hollingshead, Kelly, D (20, 14)***	1994-96
Host, Charlie, W (23)****	1994-97
Howe, Martin N., D (5)***	1959-61
Hrycun, Kelly, W (12)*	1994
Hudson, John, W (10)***	1955-57
Hudson, Lex, D (5)****	1975-78
Hudson, Barry, D (5)****	1979-82

- J -

Player	Year(s)
Jackson, Hugh, F (18)*	1976
Jackson, Bruce, G (24)*	1976

Player	Year(s)
Jacob, Richard C., W (18)*	1961
Jacobsen, Ronald A., C (16)*	1950
James, Connor, F (19)****	2001-04
James, Jack D., W-C (20, 8)***	1964-66
Janik, Craig, D (2)*	1981
John, K. Laurence, W***	1954-56
Johnson, Glenn, C (13, 7)****	1979-82
Johnson, Eric, D (5)****	1984-87
Johnston, Marshall, W-C (10)***	1961-63
Jonasson, Gerry, W (7, 10)***	1968-70
Josephson, Paul O., C (12)***	1959-61

- K -

Player	Year(s)
Kasch, Norman (24)*	1950
Keeler, Steve, D (11)*	1968
Keith, Greg, F (25)****	2001-04
Kellough, Howard J., C (7)*	1963
Kemp, Norbert A., G-C (18, 4)***	1959-61
Kenady, Chris, W (25)****	1992-95
Kenning, James D., D (5)***	1962-64
Kenny, Richard J.*	1953
Kern, James B.**	1950-51
Kester, George*	1950
Kidd, Todd, D (3)****	1996-99
Kilbey, Joseph, W (15)***	1954-56
Kirkwood, George W., G (1)**	1960-61
Klasnick, Dave, C (8, 7)****	1993-96
Klinck, Wayne, D (2)**	1958-59
Konik, George S., D (2, 3)***	1959-61
Konowalchuk, Brian, C (14)****	1991-94
Koch, Paul, D (3)****	1992-95
Koroll, Clifford E., C-W (10)***	1966-68
Kossian, William, W (4, 20)***	1952-54
Kowel, Douglas P., D (6)*	1965
Kozlowski, Frank, F (16)**	1974-75
Krieger, Bob, C-W (12)****	1971-74
Kurulak, Shawn, D (22)****	1996-99
Kvern, Norman, C (19)**	1964-65

- L -

Player	Year(s)
Laaksonen, Antti, W (10, 24)****	1994-97
Laatsch, Matt, D (27)**	2003-present
Lacomy, Gregory J., C-W (17)***	1961-63
Lamb, Jeff, C (7)****	1984-87
Lampman, Mike, W (19)***	1970-72
Larscheid, Bob, C (7)**	1983-84
Larson, Nick, D (26)*	2004-present

Player	Year(s)
Leavins, Jim, D (10)***	1981-83
Leifson, Terrance, W (18)***	1967-69
Lieg, Bob, G (14)*	1975
Lindsay, Robert A. (Sam), D (4)**	1963-64
Lindsay, J., F-D (20, 19)**	1991-92
Liprando, John, F (11)****	1980-83
Livingstone, Blair G., D (5)***	1956-58
Livingstone, Ronald, C (12)**	1963-64
Lomnes, Terence A., W (7)***	1959-61
LoPresti, Peter, G (24, 1)**	1973-74
Lozinski, Jim, G (1)*	1983
Luger, Mark, D (2)****	1991-94
Lupovich, Norman L., C (8)*	1951

- M -

Player	Year(s)
MacArthur, Ken, D (20)****	1988-90, 93
MacDonald, Murray G., W (14)***	1958-60
MacKenzie, Aaron, D (20)****	2000-03
MacMillan, John S., W (17)***	1958-60
MacPherson, Archie J. (12)*	1950
Magnan, Vince, C-W (10)****	1977-80
Magnuson, Keith, D (2)***	1967-69
Markovich, Mike, D (27)****	1989-91, 93
Marin, Harvey, G (1)*	1950
Martin, Tom, W (16)*	1983
Massier, J. Murray, C (11)**	1958-59
Masterton, William J., C (9)***	1959-61
Mathias, Scott, F (8)****	1986-89
Mathiasen, Dwight, W (9)***	1984-86
Maxwell, Pete, G (20)*	1966
Mayer, Derek, D (20, 4)***	1986-88
McAlister, Brian, D-F (2)****	1976-79
McBride, Daryn, F (16, 17)***	1987-89
McInnis, George (4)*	1950
McKinnon, Doug, D (2)**	1950-51
McLean, John, D (6)****	1992-95
McLennan, Don, D (2)****	1987-90
McMillan, Craig, D (7, 4)****	1992-95
McMillan, John, C (15)****	1984-87
McNab, Peter, W (15)***	1971-73
McWilliams, John, G (1)**	1970-71
Menzies, Doug, D (17)***	1985-87
Mercier, Don, D (4)***	1984-86
Merritt, Ken, D (3)***	1980-82
Messier, Paul, C (11)**	1977-78
Middleton, C. Barrie, W (9)***	1954-56
Miller, Ched, C (8)***	1973-75
Miller, Edward A., D-F (15)***	1951-53

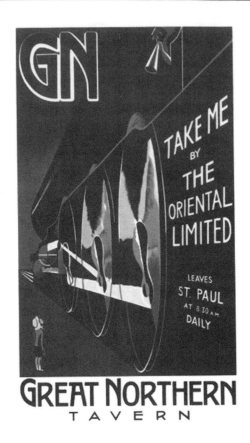
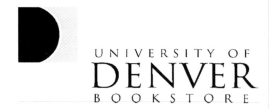

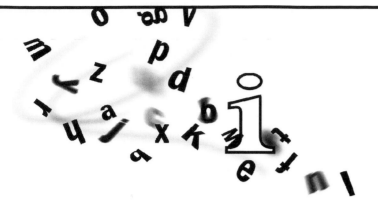

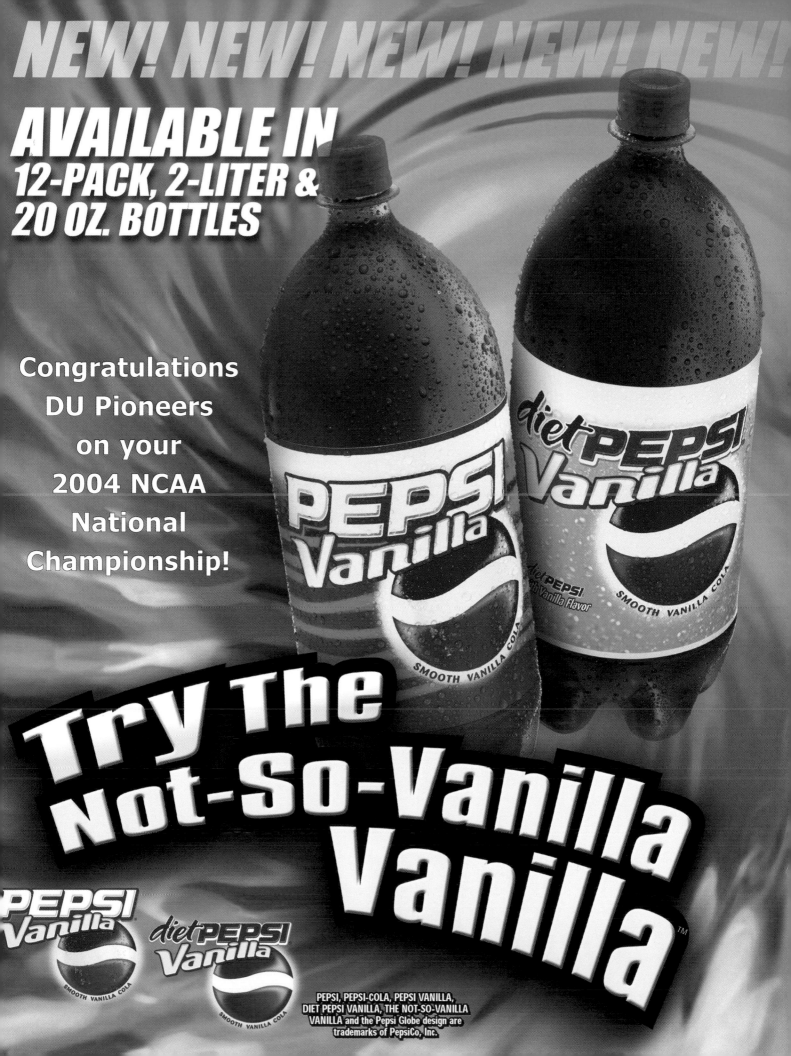

Congratulations
to the

NCAA
National
Champions

THANK YOU

ADRENALINE DESIGN
ARBY'S
BLACKJACK PIZZA
BURNSLEY HOTEL
CHICK-FIL-A
CIBER
COMCAST
COORS BREWING COMPANY
DENVER NEWSPAPER AGENCY
EGAN PRINTING COMPANY
ENTERPRISE RENT-A-CAR
FOX SPORTS NET ROCKY MTN.
FRONTIER AIRLINES
GREAT NORTHERN TAVERN

KKFN AM 950 "THE FAN"
KUSA-TV
LOEWS DENVER
MARRIOTT HOTELS
OAKWOOD HOMES
OUTBACK STEAKHOUSE
PEPSI BOTTLING GROUP
PLAYERS BENCH
QDOBA MEXICAN GRILL
TIAA CREF
ROBINSON DAIRY
ROCKY MOUNTAIN HARLEY DAVIDSON
WELLS FARGO
WINTER PARK RESORT

GREAT WIN. GREAT FRIENDS. GREAT FUTURE.
THANKS TO OUR LOYAL FAMILY OF PIONEER SUPPORTERS
IN THE BUSINESS COMMUNITY.